T5-DIH-615

Latin America and the New International Economic Order

Pergamon Titles of Related Interest

Haq Dialogue for a New Order
Haq/Streeten Development Choices for the 1980s
Meagher An International Redistribution of Wealth
Menon Bridges Across the South

UNITAR-CEESTEM Library on NIEO

Laszlo & Kurtzman Eastern Europe and the New International Economic Order
Laszlo & Kurtzman Europe and the New International Economic Order
Laszlo & Kurtzman Political and Institutional Issues of the New International Economic Order
Laszlo & Kurtzman The Structure of the World Economy and the New International Economic Order
Laszlo & Kurtzman The United States, Canada and the New International Economic ORder
Laszlo et al. The Implementation of the New International Economic Order
Laszlo et al. World Leadership and the New International Economic Order
Laszlo et al. The Objectives of the New International Economic Order
Laszlo et. al. The Obstacles to the New International Economic Order
Lozoya & Bhattacharya The Financial Issues of the New International Economic Order
Lozoya & Cuadra Africa, Middle East and the New International Economic Order
Lozoya & Bhattacharya Asia and the New International Economic Order
Lozoya & Green International Trade, Industrialization and the New International Economic Order
Lozoya & Estevez Latin America and the New International Economic Order
Lozoya & Birgin Social and Cultural Issues of the New International Economic Order
Lozoya et al. Alternative Views of the New International Economic Order
Miljan, Laszlo & Kurtzman Food and Agriculture in Global Perspective

Related Journals*

Habitat International
Socio-Economic Planning Sciences
World Development

*Free specimen copies available upon request.

Latin America and the New International Economic Order

Edited by
Jorge Lozoya
Jaime Estevez

A volume in the New International Economic Order (NIEO) Library
Published for UNITAR and the
Center for Economic and Social Studies of the Third World (CEESTEM)

Pergamon Press
NEW YORK • OXFORD • TORONTO • SYDNEY • FRANKFURT • PARIS

Pergamon Press Offices:

U.S.A.	Pergamon Press Inc., Maxwell House, Fairview Park, Elmsford, New York 10523, U.S.A.
U.K.	Pergamon Press Ltd., Headington Hill Hall, Oxford OX3 0BW, England
CANADA	Pergamon of Canada, Ltd. Suite 104, 150 Consumers Road, Willowdale, Ontario M2J 1P9, Canada
AUSTRALIA	Pergamon Press (Aust.) Pty. Ltd., P.O. Box 544, Potts Point, NSW 2011, Australia
FRANCE	Pergamon Press SARL, 24 rue des Ecoles, 75240 Paris, Cedex 05, France
FEDERAL REPUBLIC OF GERMANY	Pergamon Press GmbH, Hammerweg 6, Postfach 1305, 6242 Kronberg/Schönberg, Federal Republic of Germany

Library of Congress Cataloging in Publication Data

Main entry under title:

Latin America and the new international economic order.

(Pergamon policy studies on the new international economic order)
Bibliography: p.
Includes index.
1. Latin America—Foreign economic relations—Addresses, essays, lectures. 2. Underdeveloped areas—Economic policy—Addresses, essays, lectures. 3. International economic relations—Addresses, essays, lectures. I. Lozoya, Jorge Alberto. II. Estevez, Jaime, 1946- III. Series.
HF1480.5.L382 1980 337.8 79-27384
ISBN 0-08-025118-8

Printed in the United States of America

Contents

Preface to the UNITAR-CEESTEM NIEO Library

The present volume is one in a series of 17 books which make up the UNITAR-CEESTEM NIEO Library. While each volume covers a specific aspect of the issues that comprise the New International Economic Order and can be read independently of the others, it seems useful to provide a brief introduction to outline the scope of the entire undertaking and put this volume in its proper context.

In the winter of 1976-77, UNITAR (the United Nations Institute for Training and Research) initiated with CEESTEM (the Centro de Estudios Economicos y Sociales del Tercer Mundo, Mexico) a series of inquiries into problems and opportunities associated with the establishment of the New International Economic Order (NIEO). Both institutions agreed that the NIEO constituted one of the highest priority items on the international agenda, and that independent, objective and scholarly investigation of its objectives, obstacles, opportunities, and indicated strategies may be of great value both to the decision makers directly concerned with the negotiation of the issues, and to the international community at large. The UNITAR-CEESTEM NIEO Library is a result of the research that was undertaken by the central professional staffs of the institutes, and by their jointly formed international network of collaborators and consultants.

What are some of the reasons behind this assessment of the importance of the NIEO in contemporary economic and world affairs? Although most people know that the world economy is encountering serious difficulties on both national and international levels, few people outside a small circle of experts realize the seriousness of the problems and the breadth of their scope. Contrary to some current perceptions, the NIEO is neither a passing pressure of the poor countries on the rich, nor merely a demand for more aid and assistance. It is a process which has deep historical precedents, and an undisputed historical significance.

We need not go back further than the end of World War II to find an entire array of historical events which set the stage for the later emergence of the call for the NIEO. While these events arose from their own historical antecedents, they themselves produced the setting for the breakdown of the post-war economic system, and the widening gap between rich and poor nations.

The first and perhaps most decisive event was the liberation of the oppressed peoples of Africa and Asia, in the great wave of decolonization that swept the world in the years following World War II. The newly independent states were said to be sovereign and equal to all other states, old and new, large and small. Their admittance to the U.N. underscored this. However, the fresh political and juridical status of the new countries was far from matched by their actual economic conditions. The majority felt that their *de jure* political colonization ended only to be replaced by a *de facto* economic colonization.

The historical process which gave the majority of the world's population the status of citizens of sovereign and equal states, but left them at the same time in a situation of economic underdevelopment and dependence, triggered the "revolution of rising expectations". Desires for rapid economic growth led Third World governments into ambitious plans and programmes of national development. Most of the plans envisaged a quick repetition of the industrial growth processes of the developed world, following a path already long trodden by the countries of Latin America. When the unintended side-effects of traditional patterns of industrialization became evident -- uncontrolled growth of cities, relative neglect of rural areas and agriculture, threats to the environment, and the increasing stratification of people in modern and traditional sectors, often with serious damage to social structure and cohesion -- many of the original development strategies underwent modification. The goal of rapid economic growth was not surrendered, however. Quantitative growth targets were formally included in the official development strategies of the First and Second U.N. Development Decades (for the 1960s and the 1970s, respectively).

However, the mid-term review of the achievement of the Second Development Decade's goals showed mixed results. The greatest disappointment came in the area of agricultural production and official development aid. On the average, the U.N. official development aid targets have not even been half achieved. At the same time service charges on past loans began to put enormous pressures on developing countries' balance of payment, and world poverty showed no signs of diminishing. There was insufficient progress in commodity trade, inadequate access to the markets of developed countries, particularly for agricultural products; tariffs have escalated, especially for semi-processed and processed products, and new tariff and nontariff restrictions were introduced by many developed countries on a number of items, including textiles and leather goods. The plight of the least developed, island and land-locked developing countries, gave rise to additional concern. While some progress was achieved, for example, through the introduction of a generalized system of preferences by the developed countries, and the proposals of the Tokyo Declaration concerning multilateral trade negotiations, the negative developments weighed more heavily in the balance and created widespread dissatisfaction in the developing world.

Another set of factors came into play as well. This was the sudden and unexpected rise of Third World economic and political power. The Middle East oil embargo of 1972-73, and the subsequent fourfold increase in the price of oil created a world energy crisis. It affected all oil-importing nations, developed as well as developing. It also exhibited the dependence of the developed countries on the developing world for several major natural resources, and proved the ability of the Third World to wield economic and political power effectively. The consequences included rises in the price of food, due to the increased cost of chemical fertilizers, and further tensions between producers and consumers of raw materials. But the OPEC-type exercise of Third World economic and political power proved unable to improve the condition of the developing countries as a whole. Despite significantly higher gross resource flows from the oil-exporting to the oil-importing developing countries, the economic plight of the latter worsened due to the higher cost of energy. Developed countries found themselves beset by economic problems of their own, including not only higher oil prices but inflation, unemployment, and unused industrial capacity. Economic rates of growth slowed, while in most countries balance of payment deficits grew. Even where surpluses could still be generated, concerns focused on the domestic economy, and the political will to increase levels of aid and assistance to the Third World faltered.

Compounding the economic difficulties of the developed nations were signs of breakdown in the international monetary system which affected all countries, developed as well as developing. Amidst growing tensions between the United States, Japan, and the European Community over matters of trade, the Bretton Woods system collapsed and gave rise to a system of floating exchange rates. The value of the U.S.

dollar began to erode, creating serious difficulties for those countries which, like most of the Third World, held their reserves in dollars. The creation of Special Drawing Rights provided some access to foreign exchange independently of dollar holdings, but such access favored the countries already developed, and the rest remained seriously dissatisfied with the workings of the international monetary system. It became evident that some of the fundamental tenets of the post-war world economy were being called into question, and indeed that some had already collapsed.

The NIEO made its appearance as an international political issue in the context of this series of events. Encouraged by the success of OPEC but fearful of splintering Third World solidarity through the newly won wealth of a few of its countries, Presidents Boumedienne of Algeria and Echeverria of Mexico, among others, called for structural reforms in the international economic system. Their governments' initiative resulted in the adoption of such major U.N. resolutions as those of the Sixth and Seventh Special Session, and the Charter of Economic Rights and Duties of States. These in turn provided the impetus for a long series of declarations, resolutions, position papers and studies on various NIEO issues by the United Nations system and the international community at large.

The coming together of these historical factors was not purely coincidental. The wave of decolonization was the culmination of a long-term historical process of democratization, and the rise of the concept of universal rights for individuals and societies. It led, in turn, to a mounting desire for rapid industrialization by the newly independent countries. This met with major frustrations. But as economic interdependence intensified, as trade and markets expanded, and access to energy and raw materials became crucial to the developed world's giant economic machinery, the concentration of economic power itself was modified. It was no longer wielded by a few powerful governments but also fell into the hands of oil exporting nations and transnational corporations.

The historical process which gave birth to a host of independent nation-states placed into sharp relief the inequities of the previous economic system, and provided some of the developing countries with fresh degrees of economic leverage. Since they not only control the supply of a number of important fuels and raw materials but also absorb about 25 percent of the developed world's exports, their demands can no longer be ignored. And they insist that a healthy growth in the world economy cannot be brought about within the framework of the existing economic system.

When the General Assembly, in December, 1977 called for another Special Session in 1980 to assess progress in the establishment of the NIEO, it took a decisive step in bringing the North-South debate to the Organization, where it belongs. It created an ongoing forum for discussions and negotiation in the interim through the Committee of the Whole, which during 1978 managed to define its role and function despite earlier disagreements. Together with the work of the bodies charged with the preparation of the International Development Strategy for the Third United Nations Development Decade, the Organization created the fora for substantive progress in the area of restructuring the economic relations of developed and developing countries. Faced with mounting pressures on national economics in all parts of the world, the international community now finds itself facing a watershed decision: to make use of these fora, or to continue to use mainly bilateral and sectoral corrective measures to mitigate tensions while entrusting the resolution of problems to the mechanisms of the free market.

This decision is intimately linked to an entire array of basic questions. Among them:

The question of cost and benefit. Who will have to bear the burden of instituting NIEO and will the results be worth the sacrifices? Will benefits really accrue to the poor people to help fulfill their basic needs and will developing countries be made truly more self-reliant -- or will the main beneficiaries be the already rich elites? Will the developed countries also benefit from NIEO (a positive-sum game) or will it mainly mean the redistribution of the current stock of wealth from them to the developing countries (a zero-sum game)?

The question of legitimacy. Is the free market the basic mechanism of world trade and the best vehicle of development, or is it merely a convenient fiction to cover up the current unjust manipulations of the major economic groups?

The question of morality. Do the rich countries have a moral obligation to help the poor, and especially the poorest? Does this responsibility extend to those countries who had no historical part in the creation of poverty in the third world?

The question of political feasibility. How strongly will different organized groups in society support or oppose governmental policies aimed at the achievement of the NIEO --and how much solidarity exists in these domains internationally, among the developing and the developed countries themselves?

It is unrealistic to expect that real progress will be made on specific NIEO issues (such as official development aid, technical assistance, debt renegotiation, removal of tariff barriers, technical cooperation among developing countries, the link between SDRs and development, voting power in the World Bank and IMF, transfers of technology, regulation of transnational corporations, a system of consultations on industrialization, and restructuring the economic and social sectors of the United Nations) so long as the basic issues are not resolved and a consensus does not emerge concerning them. The NIEO can be achieved if, and only if, it is perceived that its benefits are universal and can reach all segments of the world's population (especially the neediest); if it is held that its costs do not exceed its benefits; if its regulatory mechanisms are seen to be legitimate; if some real sense of moral responsibility exists among members of the human community, and if sufficient political support is available nationally as well as internationally for the indicated measures. If one or more of these preconditions are not met, the NIEO will not be achieved; Member States will continue to practice the existing, predominantly piecemeal, ad hoc and mainly bilateral modes of adjusting to stresses and reaching compromises.

The basic purpose of the UNITAR-CEESTEM NIEO Library is to provide an independent and objective assessment of these issues, and to report its findings in time for the historic events of 1980: the Special Session of the General Assembly devoted to the assessment of progress toward the NIEO, and the immediately following regular session, during which the International Development Strategy for the 1980s and beyond (the U.N.'s Third Development Decade) is to be debated and adopted. It would clearly be an enormous waste of time and effort to enter into these negotiations without forming a clear idea of the issues that bear on their success. But reporting on them is not a simple matter of using insight and intuition; it requires painstaking and organized empirical research. The requirement is to identify the forces that operate for or against the NIEO in all parts of the world. Intuitive answers concerning its cost and benefits, legitimacy, morality, and political feasibility occur to all persons knowledgeable in these areas, but such answers tend to vary and are thus not sufficiently reliable. Expert research on the current obstacles and opportunities associated with the NIEO in the different regions of the world, and with respect to the diverse sectors of the world economy, needs to be conducted. The results of such research may shed some much needed light on the chances of success in establishing a new international economic order generally, and on the types of objectives and modes of negotiations that, in the positive case, could lead to it specifically. For although it is unlikely that a dominant consensus already exists in the world concerning the cost and benefit, legitimacy, morality, and political feasibility of the NIEO (if it did exist, the international community would probably not be experiencing the sense of frustration it has today), the precise estimation of costs versus benefits, legitimacy versus illegitimacy, morality versus indifference, and political feasibility versus futility by different societal groups could reveal highly differentiated potentials for achieving a dominant consensus in the future. Today's chaotic welter of opinions and pressures concerning the NIEO need not remain such, but could crystallize into a decisive mood favoring or opposing it. To those who object to such analysis on the grounds that economic theory, rather than wide-ranging socio-political considerations, must serve to decide the fate of NIEO, we may reply that economic theory, while relevant, is in itself over generous: it can often prove both sides of conflicting positions. Since both sides in a dispute can marshal some variety of economic theory in their defense, and no common criteria exist for assessing the relative merits of all theories, economic rationality as conveyed by economic theories becomes marginal in the negotiating process. We need to go one step deeper, inquiring into the reasons particular theories are summoned to defend particular points of view, as well as measuring the intensity of commitment to these viewpoints and the negotiating power of the parties subscribing to them.

Thus, the focus of the UNITAR-CEESTEM Library is not a given economic theory, but the perceptions and opinions underlying the positions taken by diverse actors. The configuration and strength of these perceptions and opinions will ultimately determine whether negotiations in the area of the NIEO can be successful, and if so, which strategies will have optimum chances of success.

The Library contains volumes arranged in three different series. First, there is a series of overview studies. These provide background, context, and basic reference data. They include a volume defining and classifying the principal objectives of the NIEO as agreed or debated in the United Nations and other major international fora; a volume giving an overview and assessment of alternative viewpoints on the NIEO espoused by various nongovernmental groups and researchers and different parts of the world; a third defining the most critical obstacles confronting the establishment of the NIEO; a fourth dealing with the specific problems of food and agriculture as they are debated in the framework of the United Nations. A fifth volume suggests the basic strategies which appear indicated and appropriate to accelerate progress toward the NIEO; and a final volume communicates the results of the associated UNITAR-CEESTEM International Opinion Survey of Decision-Makers and Experts on the crucial questions of the NIEO.

The second series contains geographic studies. Volumes in this series review the positions and postures of national governments and the attitudes of business, labor, the public media, and the opinion of the population at large in various nations and regions of the world. Individual volumes focus on the United States and Canada, on Western Europe, on Eastern Europe including the Soviet Union, on Asia including

Australia, on Latin America, and on Africa and the Middle East.

The third series of the NIEO Library is devoted to functional studies. Here experts give their views and assessments of such issues as the possible and the desirable structure of the world economy; of the patterns and problems of international trade and industrial development; of international financial matters, and of the associated political and institutional, as well as social and cultural problems and opportunities.

Among them, the seventeen volumes of the Library cover practically all the principal issues encountered in efforts to establish a New International Economic Order, through in-depth discussion by independent investigators, coming from different societies in different parts of the world.

The UNITAR-CEESTEM NIEO Library offers wide-ranging analyses, and sometimes divergent viewpoints, on a broad range of topics. It does not offer simplistic solutions, nor advocate one viewpoint indiscriminately over others. It seeks to illuminate the range and complexity of the issues, provide clarification of individual items, and to lend a sense of the vastness and significance of the NIEO as a whole.

It is the hope of all of us, researchers and consultants of the UNITAR-CEESTEM project on the NIEO, that our results, published as the NIEO Library, may render some service to the decisionmaker and negotiator who must cope with the problems of the international economic order, as well as to the student of international economic and world affairs, interested in further research on these topics. It is our view that the NIEO is a historically necessary, and humanly and politically appropriate attempt to create a world order that is sustainable for generations, equitable for all, and capable of meeting the most urgent needs and demands of the peoples and nations of the world community.

Ervin Laszlo
Project Director

Introduction

Latin America played a significant role in the formulation of the economic and political principles that materialized in 1974 in the struggle for the establishment of a New International Economic Order (NIEO). The Economic Commission for Latin America (ECLA) has been at the vanguard of the systematic study of the origins of underdevelopment for many years and its significance at the birth of UNCTAD is well known. Latin American countries also played an important role during UNCTAD III in Santiago, and it was the Mexican initiative at that conference that originated the Charter of Economic Rights and Duties of States.

This energetic and vital participation by Latin America in global issues has its roots in the social and political experience of the region, which is characterized by a complex history in the creation and growth of independent nation states, common traditions, and a common language. The general level of economic progress achieved by several of the Latin American countries identifies the region as more developed than most other areas of the Third World.

For over 150 years the region has generated democratic institutions and proposed imaginative programs of national development. However, in the last decades Latin America's dependency on the United States has created a contrast to other areas of the developing world that have been able to diversify their political and economic linkages.

At the same time, even though economic growth has occurred in many Latin American countries, the internal differences with respect to income distribution and access to social welfare have worsened. Participative democracy, a basic goal of the New International Economic Order, and a deep-rooted ideal in the philosophical tradition of Latin America, is not at the present time an element in many of the political systems of the region. On the contrary, in several countries there exists a dangerous, repressive, and authoritarian rule.

In the center of Latin America's crisis is the failure of the developmental model based on import substitution as well as the inability of the region to satisfactorily defend an independent role in the new international division of labor. With this failure comes the danger that countries with higher levels of socioeconomic development will attempt to negotiate bilaterally to solve their economic difficulties and adjust themselves to the present restructuring of the market economies, to the detriment of the majority of the member states of the region. Bilateralism would have a negative impact on the region by reducing its negotiating strength and capacity as a bloc. One of the basic impediments to the coordination of agreements at regional and interregional levels is the tendency toward bilateralism and its neutralizing internal and political effects.

In the Caribbean subregion of Latin America, the process of decolonization has given rise to the creation of a group of countries with little economic viability. In some cases, recently established duty free zones serve the interests of transnational corporations more than they alleviate the socioeconomic needs of the country.

The generalized economic crisis of the Third World has accentuated the characteristics of Latin American dependency. This is revealed in the tendency to strengthen the region's role as a raw material exporter and in the increasing percentage of its actors in the industrial sectors that have become attached to transnational corporations. The parallel crisis of the international monetary and financial systems worsens the overall situation.

The transfer of financial resources for development has not been effective in achieving the United Nations growth targets. To this must be added difficulties associated with external debt as well as the ever-growing pressures and conditions accompanying refinancing. In real terms, the Latin American region has financed the development of industrial countries due to the ultimately negative results of the financial transfers.

The acute disequilibrium and instability of the international monetary system, the persistence of the inflationary processes, the lack of confidence in the role played by the international financing institutions, the increasing predominance of private interests in the financial markets and the consequent lack of control on the part of international bodies in the creation of international liquidity, have all been identified as obstacles to the New International Economic Order. These, along with the unlikely possibility of using special drawing rights (SDRs) as the main asset of reserves of the monetary system, the failure to realize the SDR/Aid Link, and the current instability of the international exchange system have been the main inhibiting financial factors in the establishment of the NIEO in the region. It is essential, therefore, to undertake assistance strategies that avoid subordination to the will of granting countries and to implement these strategies within the framework of the United Nations.

At a meeting in Mexico (January 1979) the contributors to the UNITAR/CEESTEM Library on the NIEO suggested a review of the power structure of the international financial system as a whole, not only in relation to their voting mechanism, in order to be able to adjust those institutions to the ever-changing and complex realities of international finance and development. The creation of a Central World Bank truly attached to the United Nations was also proposed at the discussions.

The Latin American experts advocated the creation of an international currency based on a group of raw materials and the creation of buffer stocks in order to avoid price fluctuations. Price indexation, of Latin American and developing world exports to the exports of goods and capital of industrialized countries, was also suggested as long as it was to benefit Latin America rather than the transnational corporations.

In the area of international trade the experts reported little progress in the establishment and further development of regional integration. Transnational corporations exercise a tight control on the important natural resources of the region and also on the marketing of many products, including those in the Integrated Commodity Program. At the same time, the official protection of sectors of low competitiveness in developed countries hampers access of developing country manufactures to the international market.

Although there appears to be a global increase in the volume of Latin American trade, commercial relations between the enterprises of the developed countries and their subsidiaries in the developing world make it difficult to identify the real benefit of such an increase to the countries of the region.

In general there is a poor integration in the industrial apparatus, which concentrates on the production of goods of low technology, while there is increasing activity in the subcontracting industries that are not fully integrated into the productive domestic system but are concerned with reducing the cost of labor for transnational enterprises.

Although it does not constitute a solution to all of the more urgent problems, it appears necessary to advocate the creation of producers' associations that may proceed in the timely distribution of goods, and be used as tools to financially support research and development.

The developmental models present in Latin America have made the achievement of the targets of economic growth and the redistribution of political and social power extremely difficult. Conditions of employment, real per capita income, and access to social security have been aggravated by these models. As a consequence of inadequate educational systems, the region has been unable to provide effectively for the needs of a young and growing population. Associated with these educational problems is the condition of the increasing migration of scientific and technical experts toward the industrial countries. In addition, in the case of several Latin American countries, there is a dispersion of experts and intellectuals created by current political conditions.

In contrast to previous decades, there is both a lack of interest in international affairs and a failure of the political will needed to advance the process of internal change and international cooperation. At the same time traditional rivalries survive with the potential for confrontation still present in some areas of the region.

Yet, the region seems to be evolving toward a new stage of democratization that is related to a more significant and positive role in the international scene. This tendency has mainfested itself in different ways. There is hope for positive change in Central America; there is revitalization of the representative system in several South American countries; there is expectancy about renewed political participation. At the same time, the Caribbean is slowly moving toward internal integration and regional dialogue. This means that lasting long-term achievements can materialize in the region only if the new economic order enables states to choose development patterns that allow broad political democratization while coping with the problems of income accumulation and distribution.

The editors wish to acknowledge the permanent support of Davidson Nicol, Executive General of UNITAR, and of B.F. Osorio-Tafall, Director General of the Center for Economic and Social Studies of the Third World (CEESTEM), as well as the enthusiastic leadership of Ervin Laszlo in the realization of the UNITAR/CEESTEM Project.

1 The Transformation of Latin America

Enrique Oteiza
Susana Schkolnik
Jorge Fontanals
Fernando Porta

The framework in which the Latin American countries presently figure in the negotiations for the New International Economic Order is characterized by a series of contradictions. These contradictions are the result of the various development experiences undergone by the different countries, as well as of their achievements. Nevertheless, two essential aspects define a common characteristic for the analysis of development.

First of all, it is important to consider the influence of capitalism's development on a world scale, particularly in its current phase of intensification and internationalization. This phase is particularly highlighted by the various forms of domination of international capital. As a result, the importance of the role of the transnational corporations, the most advanced form of capitalism during this phase, lies in the degree to which they have caused the internationalization of dependent economies. This phenomenon finds a correlative in the growing association of the local elites with international capital.

The transnational corporation is characterized by a) a high degree of concentration of capital; b) professional management; c) operations designed on a world scale; d) capacity to generate and monopolize technology; e) structures of production to be found in central and periphery countries; f) information and electronic information processing with almost instantaneous communication and decision processes that are centralized in the developed capitalist countries; and g) preferential access to many national markets.

The second aspect of this economic phase of development lies in the process of structural and social changes carried out in the dependent economies. The development of capital since the postwar period meant, for all Latin American countries in varying degrees, a model of a concentrative and excluding nature that revealed evident inequalities. The development process tended to superimpose the conflicts within the bourgeois factions over those in the salaried sectors. What arose from the accelerated industrialization which characterized this period was a large and growing urban proletariat not only in the secondary but also in the tertiary sectors. In some cases, this proletariat created a majority within the composition of the labor force.

These changes in the social structure as well as the increasingly serious nature of the contradictions provoked by the introduction of the development model, radicalized Latin American political development. Gradually, popular movements began to question the social and political order on which the accumulation of capital was based, going beyond demands pertaining to income distribution.

The dependent industrialization model gave priority to the development of the production of consumer goods. This converted the economy's external sector into the main supplier of the material means of production. Export sectors, as foreign exchange producers, acted as replacements for this structural insufficiency. The bourgeois factions linked to the traditional export sectors continued to maintain an important amount of economic and political power. In some countries until the 1930 crisis, and in others until the beginning of the postwar period, these traditional sectors had been predominant in the nation state and in the development of the primary-exporter model. This circumstance created frequent conflicts and critical situations in the external sector of the economy which accompanied Latin American industrial growth.

Within this same area of change, what must be emphasized is the redefinition of the characteristics of the domestic market and its growth model with respect to the successive phases adopted by industrialization. The process presents two permutations that have taken place. The transition toward a hierarchical domestic market related to the diversification of consumption in the relatively minor consumer sectors with high purchasing power brought to a standstill and reversed the diffusion processes of consumption. This was due to an expansion in the number of consumers, which accompanied the first steps of import-substitution types of industrialization. The new accumulation model is closely linked to the processes of regression in income distribution and the penetration of transnational capital in the most advanced sectors of the economy (devoted to the production of durable consumer goods), designed in the market economy countries.

Hence, we see a growing structural need for orienting a part of industrial production toward external markets - not simply as the solution to a distribution problem of potentially exportable balances, but rather as a more relevant form of carrying out production. On another level, this process arises as an answer to the problem of an expansion in industrial production which will satisfy the growing need for international foreign exchange. This need is seen in frequent crises in the balance of payments.

The process of intense concentration and centralization of capital favors the consolidation of sectors of the local economy that are strongly concentrated and which gradually become more closely associated with transnational capital. Thus, the interests of these sectors are redefined.

In this process of broadening the sphere of dominion and action of capital, and in the redefinition of the nature of the domestic market, necessary for the present stage of reproduction and growth of capital, the nonconcentrated factions of national capital have been weakened. These factions are sometimes a mouthpiece for political projects of a progressive nature in the framework of a moderately redistributive economic strategy.

The process has been accompanied by greater state participation in the economic sphere, in the expansion of the infrastructure as well as in political action in the mediation of problems and in the reproduction of the structures of control. These phenomena have imposed modifications on the functions and structure of the state. Particular forms of state capitalism have been developed, whose most advanced expression can be seen in the expansion of state economic production in close connection with transnational and local capital.

In turn, the need for state intervention as well as the capacity for such interventions has grown with respect to the general economic situation. In some cases, this dynamic of state intervention has given rise to a governing technobureaucratic sector which, in the absence of democratic forms of political representation, has gradually taken on the direct function of ordering the reproduction of capital. In this process new contradictions are generated when the need for a greater concentration is challenged by the specific interests of specific national and foreign economic factors whose interests may be ignored or harmed by the decisions of the state bureaucracy.

These processes at the state level are clearly visible in the more advanced continental links and even in those that have attained an intermediate level of development in their productive forces. Likewise, be it in a partial or diffuse form, these processes can be seen in almost all other countries in the region. The differences observed in their specific manifestations, of which many diverse politicoeconomic movements are a reflection, find their explanation in the articulation of both the "external" and the "internal" aspects of the political and economic dynamic.

This advantageous insertion in the international division of labor, governed by the expansion of transnational capital, has emphasized the question of control of the system which results in the subordination of society as a whole to the specific aims of certain sectors of the economy. The model of political domination, and the internal and external alliances which support it, give the appearance of stability while, at the same time, the contradictions inherent in this model are hidden so that no open manifestations of the conflict will occur. Without the disappearance of the characteristics of a strongly repressive state, it is possible to observe only pseudodemocratic forms in the current Latin American political regimes. This occurs when the exploited groups lack political and organized development.

On the other hand, situations exist where the huge concentrations of capital face serious difficulties in converting economic dominance into political predominance. There are also other situations in which this model of production is no longer relevant to meet the present needs of world capital accumulation. At the same time, the political and organized growth of popular movements represents a sharpening and a political radicalization of social conflicts. In these cases, the outcome is often a military state that is nonparticipatory and strongly repressive.

2 Latin America and the New International Economic Order

Carlos Arriola

A broad consensus seems to exist on the need to create a New International Economic Order. Nevertheless, this consensus does not imply a systematic knowledge of what this order should consist of, what the principles and ideas are which animate it, and what are the means to achieve it.

The obstacles preventing the implementation in Latin America of the 1974-75 United Nations resolutions on the NIEO are multiple and varied in nature. for this reason, we shall restrict ourselves to noting the main trends and avoid the risk of useless generalizations.

The Gradual Abandonment of Ideas and Models of Autonomous Development

After the second half of the 1960s there was a rapid transformation of the production process in the more industrially developed Latin American countries. This transformation was characterized by the internationalization of Latin American industry, led by transnational enterprises which have replaced the national entrepreneurs by converting them into minor partners. The system of production of the most advanced capitalist countries of the periphery is thus based on the close association of the multinationals, the state, and the national entrepreneur.

According to Helio Jaguaribe,(1) one of the consequences of this process is the abandonment of ideas and efforts aimed at achieving greater autonomy in the development process, although the myths and rites of classical nationalism persist, as well as the accentuation of trends toward a greater dependence on the international economy, especially on that of the United States.

The Greater Heterogeneity of Latin American Countries

Despite the fact that a Latin American community has been talked about since independence was achieved in the nineteenth century, the differences between the countries of the region have become more noticeable. Therefore, it must be taken into account that the interests of the Latin American countries are not always complementary, and in many circumstances are even contrary.

Besides the differences in the level of development of the countries of the region, it is relevant to consider the fact that the difficulties experienced by the international economy will tend to accentuate the national differences, with the result that Latin American governments will refuse to take on commitments of regional solidarity which may reduce their freedom of action or impose collective discipline on them.

The Lack of Ideological Pluralism

The growing diversity in the continent has resulted neither in a real ideological pluralism, nor in a significant measure of respect for the development models adopted by other countries. This condition prevents any idea of solidarity and cooperation from emerging, let alone any ideas of integration. In Latin America a progressive socialist country may coexist with a military government with an anachronistic cold war mentality. Between these two extremes are found different options, although military and authoritarian governments predominate.

In this respect, it may be mentioned that ideas for Latin American integration, and the hopes raised by the signing of the Montevideo Treaty, have been greatly diminished. On the other hand, trends towards bilateralism are acquiring a greater dynamism, and as a result, the multilateral Latin American Free Trade Association (LAFTA), the Andean Pact, and the Central American Common Market have become stagnant. However, it must be taken into account that new signs of revitalization are emerging. The Andean Group has shown a relevant degree of commitment in terms of the support offered to the new democratic trends in Central America. It has also reinforced its juridical structure. The Latin American Economic System (SELA) is a relatively new instrument offering some basis of coordination of future Latin American cooperation efforts.

The ideological diversity, the lack of political will, and the difficulties of the present economic situation have resulted in a tense situation which threatens confrontations, including armed ones.

The Absence of a Clear View of Latin America's Role in the World

The weakening of regional and subregional mechanisms for cooperation, and the return by the majority of Latin American countries to less than glorious isolation, has resulted in a lack of concern for international affairs. With the exceptions of Brazil and Cuba, which have a clear idea of their external objectives, the majority of Latin American countries have adopted a passive attitude, trying to adapt themselves as well as possible to the changing circumstances of the international scene. In an article published at the end of 1977, Claudio Veliz speaks of "extraordinary incompetence, exceptional lack of professionalism, and an embarrassing poverty of initiative in the field of international relations," and points out that the "de facto" governments of South America look down on diplomacy and the professionalism of foreign service.(2)

This lack of interest in international affairs and the withdrawal of professionals from international relations have resulted in a lack of vision concerning Latin America's role in the world and a consequent reduction in the weight of the region as a negotiating bloc.

The Thesis of the Incompatibility of Interests Between Latin America and the Rest of the Third World

There are several authors who consider that the association of Latin American countries with those of the rest of the Third World is not realistic. For instance, the German economist Wolfgang Konig, who has worked in Latin America for many years, states that "the nucleus of the demands listed in the NIEO are not of absolute priority for Latin America, and these demands are of secondary importance compared to the need for the continent to reshape its relations with the United States."

The main argument used is that Latin America has a relatively diversified economic structure, with a greater, more accentuated qualitative and quantitative dependence on the industrialized countries. To recover its rate of growth, Konig considers it necessary to strengthen the industrial base through the expansion and diversification of exports of manufactured products. Consequently, Latin America depends, to a larger degree than other regions of the Third World, on its industrial links with the developed countries. In the case of a confrontation, the countries of Latin America have a lot more to lose than some of the nonaligned countries.

According to Konig, the lack of a Latin American position on international economic affairs and ambivalent ideas on the NIEO arise not from individual personalities but from changes which have taken place in the economic structure of the region.(3)

A variant of this thesis is the notion that the solution to the problems of underdevelopment basically depends on the internal decisions made by the countries of the Third World. In his contribution to this project the Argentinian economist Aldo Ferrer considers that fundamental changes in the behavior of the trilateral system toward the periphery are not to be expected in the foreseeable future. Ferrer specifies three basic reasons for this: the marginal character of the periphery with respect to the central concerns of the trilateral system; second, the internal nature of the problems of underdevelopment and the "unavoidable" responsibility of every country to overcome these problems; and third, the fact that the transformation of center-periphery relations depends fundamentally upon the decisions of the developed nations. Ferrer concludes that "the problems of underdevelopment cannot be solved within the limits of the North-South dialogue, neither can the countries of the Third World make claims on the trilateral system for decisions for which the responsibility lies basically with themselves."

Within this perspective Ferrer considers that the potential for autonomy in Latin America has broadened substantially. The capacity to take advantage of this potential autonomy depends on the size of each country, on its level of development, and on its capacity for accumulation. It also depends on the objectives outlined by each country, as well as the efficiency and political backing of strategies aimed at promoting accelerated, independent development.(4)

The Lack of Consensus About How to Negotiate With the Central Countries

Latin American experts are divided on the problem of how negotiations between the countries of the center and the periphery should be approached. The main positions which they have taken are those of "global confrontation" and "thematic approximation."

As regards the first position, some experts, such as Luciano Tomassini, consider that confrontation between countries of the center and the periphery is inevitable since the most powerful of the rich countries "are getting used to making joint decisions at the highest level." The "spirit of Rambouillet" is weakening the position of the countries of the periphery, since, as it appears, the United States has begun to agree to share the tutelary power over the international economy which it had exercised practically single-handed in the last three decades with the other large capitalist powers, and because of this a "system of shared responsibilities of the large powers in the running of the international economy" will arise. In light of this, Tomassini adds, intermediate positions must be formed to allow problems to be located and common objectives to be defined in certain areas or in certain special fields. These intermediate positions would be composed of peripheral countries which could get together in a rapid and effective way to make decisions aimed at obtaining a power of veto every time that the basic interests of the periphery were at stake.(5)

Other experts consider that the confrontation between the countries of the center and the periphery in the different international gatherings has gone no further than oratorical exercises, and has not resulted in agreements which allow progress to be made in the creation of a new international economic order. For this reason, they tend to approach negotiations from a sectoral point of view. This proposal has been drawn up mainly by the countries of the center, but it also attracts some Latin American experts. Celso Furtado, in a study presented recently,(6) considered this way of approaching the problem of negotiations to be "advisable." The main suggestions of this proposal are that a) each issue should be negotiated separately; b) a forum should be set up for each topic; c) the resulting agreements should not be grouped together in the same package; d) only the directly interested parties should participate in the respective negotiations; and e) procedures should be adopted which compensate for the different negotiating capacities of the parties.

The Limited Knowledge of Political Evolution in the Countries of the Center

A final fact which deserves mention is the small number of experts in the countries of the periphery who have an adequate knowledge of the changes taking place in the advanced countries and in the international scene. The present Secretary General of the Economic Commission for Latin America (ECLA), Enrique Iglesias, has, like many others who study these problems, called attention to the fact that all the important changes come from the North, and for this reason it is extremely important to review theories of dependency and to design new working instruments in the light of the changes taking place every day in the more advanced countries. Only in this way will it be possible to adopt new strategies to improve the participation of the countries of the periphery in the international system.

The enumeration of the above problems does not lead to optimism. The majority of the obstacles mentioned have no easy solution. They arise from the lack of political will of the majority of the governments of the continent to carry out, or at least to initiate, processes leading to internal change, or to encourage processes of regional and subregional cooperation. Nevertheless, there is reason to believe that many of the obstacles stated above are part of the existing economic situation, and to hope that Latin America will recover the political will to overcome the problems which it faces.

There is no doubt that the region has economic and human resources which can be mobilized whenever the political will to do so exists. One of the most appropriate ways appears to be to approach negotiations on different aspects of the NIEO in an individual fashion, grouping only those countries which have a direct interest. Naturally this "thematic approximation" runs the risk of destroying the spirit and content of the NIEO. For this reason analysis and discussion of the global problems which concern the international community must proceed simultaneously with consideration of problems such as the reform of the United Nations system, disarmament and international security, technology transfer, protection of the environment, food production, and regulating the activities of transnational corporations.

NOTES

(1) Helio Jaguaribe, "El Informe Linowitz y las relaciones Estados Unidos-America Latina," Estudios Internacionales 40 (October-December 1977): 53.

(2) Claudio Veliz, "Errores y omisiones: notas sobre la politica exterior de los paises de America Latina durante los ultimos diez anos," Estudios Internacionales 40 (October-December 1977): 5-12.

(3) Wolfgang Konig, "America Latina y un Nuevo Orden Economico Internacional," Nueva Politica 1, no. 2 (October 1976-March 1977): 226.

(4) Aldo Ferrer, "The Structure of the World Economy: a Southern Perspective," in The Structure of the World Economy and the New International Economic Order, ed. Ervin Laszlo and Joel Kurtzman (New York: Pergamon Press, 1980).

(5) Luciano Tomassini, "Falencias y falacias: notas sobre el estudio de las relaciones Norte-Sur," Estudios Internacionales 40 (October-December 1977): 120-129.

(6) Celso Furtado, "El reordenamiento de la economia mundial," Nueva Politica 1, no. 4 (October 1976-March 1977): 55.

3 The Political Systems of Latin America: From Neoauthoritarianism to Participative Democracy

Juan Carlos Portantiero

CRISIS AND RECONSTRUCTION OF THE INTERNATIONAL ECONOMIC ORDER

We are witnessing a universal turning point, comparable to the depression of 1929 or the effects of World War II. We are currently in a transition between two stages, in which a readjustment of the relations between world forces is taking place, with the particular characteristic that the number of parties involved is greater, more varied, and more complex. For the first time, the geopolitical world encompasses the whole geographical mass. This universalization of political relationships is a result of the postwar system, which is itself currently entering a cycle of destabilization.

More than any other, the current crisis is a crisis in the balance of power; that is to say, it clearly reflects the behavior of its social protagonists, rather than obeying so-called fatalistic laws of historical development.

The future of our world (a future which is close at hand) will depend on the nature of relations between those who are today the principal protagonists in the international arena, which has become significantly more fragmented. The realities of social and international relations enable us to recognize the following groups:

1) A hegemonic block, composed of those countries with a market economy (capitalist)
2) A block of countries with planned economies (socialist)
3) The periphery. (Other authors, such as Wallerstein and Gunder Frank, propose a redefinition of classification, according to which

in the "economic world" today there are two subdivisions which identify with the capitalist "center": the "semiperiphery" composed of those countries with planned and market economies which hold an intermediate position in the international division of labor, and the "periphery" into which fall most of the underdeveloped countries of the Third World. This classification, on which I will elaborate further, proves highly useful in understanding some aspects of the current reshaping of the world economic order.)

These groups are increasingly brought together by the presence of one of the central elements which characterizes our present age: the transnational corporations, which are the direct economic agents of the present process of the internationalization of the productive structure. We will pay particular attention to those companies commited to a process of "specialization" in the international productive system, which has expanded in the last decade. Their influence vis-a-vis any possible alternative reorganization of the world economic order is decisive in that such an option could be in their own interests.

The transnational corporations under consideration sprang up and were developed in the capitalist group; yet, realistically, they cannot be tied to those societies and states in which they have their headquarters, since their interests do not always coincide with those of their countries of origin. Furthermore, each of these three groupings has its own internal differences: principal and secondary centers, and in the case of the periphery, notable internal differences in the style and level of development of each country.

It has already been said that, insofar as politics has become universalized, in a world not only international but transnational, the presence of this multitude of protagonists (with varying degrees of power) suggests that the crisis concerns the balance of power in various projects which have different goals and interests. As never before, the crisis, and its possible solutions, are defined in political terms.

In the geopolitical arena, these conflicts have been categorized by a dual polarity: North-South and East-West. This essay will deal with problems relating to the "South"; that is, the subsystems of peripheral societies which are journalistically referred to as the Third World. Within the latter, this essay will focus on a specific region: Latin America. Yet such terms as Third World or even Latin America make better metaphors than analytical instruments, since they have more than one meaning. Within the subsystem, whose greatest forum is the Movement of Non-

Aligned Nations, one finds vastly disparate levels of economic, social, cultural, and political development, and, therefore, greatly different options for joining and reshaping the world system. A very important factor in this disparity is, undoubtedly, the potential capacity which each country within the peripheral group has to offer in order to renegotiate its role in the newly created order with the center groups. One has only to note the imbalance in international weight, based on the disparity of resources, between the oil-producing countries and the rest of the Third World.

The problem is, therefore, a complex one. Having stressed the disparities in levels of development and in possession of vital resources between countries, one could just as well refer to the dissimilarities between the prevailing political systems or traditional cultural structures. The patterns of Eastern and Western values (real, despite the perverse use made of them during the cold war) split the peripheral subsystems, for example, by setting Latin America apart from other areas whose cultural traditions proved more resistant to the impact of colonization.

Both the social traits of the ruling elites and the characteristics and traditions of the working classes in each of the countries are elements which have to be taken into consideration when trying to explain this diversity. It remains clear, however, that the wish to eradicate these differences is purely analytical. Insofar as they set apart the forgotten humanity which makes up three quarters of the world, they represent a historically unified set of problems. This unity cannot, however, be considered as the beginning, but rather as the end of the argument which enables one better to determine the real set of problems. It is in moments of crisis and change, as at present, that each society tries to jockey for position in the inevitable reconstruction of the world system. Surely, this will not have to happen in a catastrophic way inasmuch as neither a world war nor world revolution are probable. It is the analysis of these differences which will provide a more rewarding way toward a realistic investigation that would result in a synthesis of the problem.

These considerations, relative to the need to break down vast sociopolitical categories of the Third World type, would, in my opinion, prove particularly relevant to the analysis of Latin America. The Latin American case is important insofar as it shows a particular form of interrelationship between economics and politics, and between society and state, in this crucial transition period which the whole continent is experiencing as part of the readjustment undertaken by the whole periphery in order to generate a new international order. Latin America has retained, within the Third World, the peculiarity of having already completed some stages along the road to development, beginning with its early creation of sovereign juridical entities in the first half of the nineteenth century. Clearly, in no way is it suggested that this evolution, which began more than one and a half centuries ago at the time of political independence, should be passed on immediately to all the other peripheral nations as if it were a mirror into which these nations should look to determine their future. Though it is common knowledge that history is not unilinear, the stage reached by the more important societies in Latin America suggests to the researcher a set of ideas which are especially interesting in relation to the way in which the periphery has integrated the world market, a market currently in crisis and in need of redefinition. In turn, this redefinition is neither singular nor neutral and implies a social choice between alternatives.

Latin American societies obtained their independence from Spain and Portugal and from their initial function as mere suppliers of raw materials; they moved into a second stage as a direct result of the new openness of the world economies, caused by the crash in 1929 and subsequently reinforced by the effects of World War II. Together with strong protectionist legislation, the region's more important countries undertook an accelerated program of industrialization through import substitution processes which coincided symmetrically with the central states' adoption of export substitution.

Exploiting the conditions created by the protectionist legislation introduced by Latin American governments during the thirties (particularly in Colombia, Mexico, and Argentina), foreign capital changed its traditional role. In conjunction with domestic capital, it established itself increasingly in light industry which aimed to supply previously imported consumer goods to virtually captive markets. This caused structural changes within these societies: the creation, strengthening, or subjugation of certain classes, strata, and groups of the population; the emergence of new relations between state and society through the ever increasing diversity of roles of the former as much in the social field as main agent of income redistribution, as in the purely economic field as owner of public services and manufacturing industries.

One of the purposes of this study is to precisely analyze these morphological changes, which are occurring in the most important countries of the region as a direct result of the crisis in the plan for industrialization through "public development" conceived and implemented between the mid-thirties and the late fifties. The project was linked, at the time, to monetary ties between the Latin American economies and the world market, a result of the depression and the war. This enabled certain countries with more favorable internal market conditions to achieve semiautonomous growth.

Already in the mid-fifties, and especially after the boom created by the Korean War, this unusual situation started to disappear, seriously hindering the type of development hitherto undertaken. The new world situation, increasingly characterized by a transnationalization of economy, began to aim at an economic growth, in accordance with chosen patterns, which was incompatible with the process of redistribution of social and political power, as it had been undertaken. Thus began the so-called crisis of populism (the relevance of this merits discussion) and a crisis in the type of development which supported the forms of government which had on the whole enlarged considerably the mechanism of social and political participation. The crisis is therefore also one of the liberal representative forms of government.

To varying degrees, and in an attempt to adapt to the new circumstances of world economics, neoauthoritarian governments are emerging, violently restricting the political system, even in countries which have reached a considerable level of political development. In these instances the countries have begun on a downhill path to acute institutional regression.

It cannot be said that all the countries in the region, having reached similar levels of integration into the world economy, have opted for the same political answers to the readjustments prompted by the power elites. Mexico, Colombia, and Venezuela, for example, maintain an institutional continuity within the framework of liberal constitutionalism. The existence of this diversity must make the analyst wary of falling into oversimplified determinism. It is nonetheless true that when the insatiable need of the elites to readjust their position within the world system coincides with a political crisis (the origins of which can never be solely due to shifts in the economy), the forces of democratic liberalization become unable to resist the change and are thus ultimately destroyed. It is therefore the variable in the causal chain, i.e., the presence or absence of a political crisis, which serves to associate the changes in the pattern of economic development with the authoritarian types of changes which occur in the political system. A legitimate concern, however, leads one to wonder in what way certain economic and social development plans favor, more than others, the unleashing of a political crisis and the subsequent emergence of authoritarian trends.

What has happened in Latin America in the last 25 years? A fitting answer is given by ECLA (Economic Commission for Latin America) in a document issued by its executive secretary:

> In truth, many, if not the majority of Latin Americans, do not understand the profound changes which have taken place in this field in the last 25

> years. The changes have been substantial both in their magnitude and their structural composition. Let us recall some representative figures: In 1950, the total national product (NP) of Latin America (measured at the 1970 dollar value) amounted to 60 billion dollars. In 1974, this figure rose to 220 billion, nearly a four fold increase over 1950, at a time when Europe was one of the most industrialized areas in the world and some of its nations were among the leading world economic powers....On the other hand, the larger Latin American economies have already achieved a size comparable to that of the major European economies in the 1950s.

However, alongside this "extraordinary display of productive force," the document stresses the existence of another dimension.

> It must not be thought that we are overlooking an aspect which tarnishes (and without doubt dramatically) these prospects and achievements. I refer to the fact that a large section of the Latin American people has not been able to take part in this process, either as active elements of change or as the beneficiaries of the breakthroughs which have favored other groups. Contrastingly, the high income groups have been able to reproduce and enjoy the consumer patterns which the industrialized nations took a long time to attain....Of the average increase in per capita income of 100 dollars during the sixties, the per capita share in the poorest 20 percent of the population was only 2 dollars....We are today some 300 million Latin Americans. 100 million live in conditions of extreme poverty and of these 65 million live in rural areas, on the periphery of the markets and lacking the minimum culture which would enable them to imagine an existence different to that which they have been living for generations. On the other hand, those who have moved to the cities, even if they have received some of the leftovers of modern society, have on the whole, been relegated to shoe string poverty which contrasts violently with the prosperity of the large urban centers which are being erected all over the width and breadth of our America....And all this is not due to lack of resources.(1)

What has happened in Latin America is tantamount to a flat denial of the usual theories of the political sociology of the fifties, according to which economic development, social modernization, and political democracy were intertwined with what was called "the optimistic equation." This positive correlation between economic growth and development, stated in an enlightened vision of historical progress, failed to materialize. Having reached a certain point, the chosen form of development has come up against its own limits; development gives rise to a growth in participation, manifest in a chaotic pluralization of demands, which in turn cause stagnation, inflation, and a feeling of threat to the position of the elites. The institutional order wavered, and from this point on the authoritarian solutions emerged as an answer to the political crisis.

Raul Prebisch has submitted the behavior patterns of "peripheral capitalism" to close scrutiny, in several recent works concluding that economic development in the abstract is not automatically capable of providing an increase in participation or a better distribution of resources, be they economic, social, cultural, or political. On the contrary, certain forms of development, such as those carried out in Latin America, are bringing about a concentration of income and an ever increasing exclusion of the great majority of the population, while favoring extravagant consumption of goods of ever greater sophistication.

This distortion, peculiar to a style of development in which lifestyles and behavior patterns are linked to the control which transnational companies exert over consumption in peripheral countries, is the arena in which the current political and social conflicts of Latin America are taking place. With the end of the first phase of industrialization in the mid-fifties, and through import substitution, the decline in the productive capacity of the peripheral countries' domestic markets will progressively worsen, while the economies of the central states are speeding up the transnationalization of production. In the wake of 25 years which were among the most glittering in the history of capitalism, the crisis which began at the beginning of the 1970s has brought to the fore the need for a reorganization of the world economic system. The rich countries took over an initiative, which, with other aims, had been started by the Third World over a decade previously. Over and above the recommendations of international organizations, it is a fact that a restructuring of the world economic system is currently in progress and that a return to the type of national-populist economic models which underwent crisis in Latin America no longer seems viable.

The new, more "open" age, seen in the context of a recession in the world economy, implies a redefinition of the international division of labor. Economic booms and repressions will alternate over a long period of time. To some authors,(2) these moments (_trends seculaires_ according to French historiography) are particularly decisive for the so-called semiperipheral countries (that is, those who occupy an intermediate position in the international system), since important repositioning on an international scale tends to occur during such transitions. This grouping of semiperipheral countries, which in the case of Latin America would be composed of those countries with greater development, can achieve certain advantages which are not within the reach of the strictly peripheral countries, that is, the group composed of the most underdeveloped countries.

A logical and empirical explanation of the emergence of the authoritarianism which exists in many of the most developed countries in Latin America should not be isolated from the consideration of the elites' need to accumulate power so as to enable them to readjust the internal conditions of their societies, in their search for easier access to higher positions in a changing world system. Hence, the picture becomes more complicated. The contradiction between semiperipherals and peripherals (as well as the competitiveness within the countries of the former, since all of them will not be able to enjoy the advantages of the moment) forces one to introduce a note of skepticism when evaluating the prospects of setting up a homogeneous pressure front for some of these countries vis-a-vis the central economic groups. The problem which the subordinates have in trying to present a unified front when confronting the central groups shifts the emphasis from their relations with the outside world to power relations within each country. In a word, if in the course of this "epoch-making" crisis, the subordinate societies are not capable of redefining internally their aims, values, and power structures which give meaning to the development projects and lifestyles which they propose, then the emerging new international system will retain the same characteristics of inequality which it has at present.

THE NEW INTERNATIONAL ECONOMIC ORDER SEEN AS A PROBLEM OF CHOICE BETWEEN ALTERNATIVES

What do we mean when we speak of a New International Economic Order? Certainly not a fact of life, but an option, resulting from a choice between alternatives.

One cannot say at which point these disputed alternatives become clear - particularly in the case of a possible alternative for subordinate countries - but it is a fact that any discussion of this type cannot ignore the huge bibliography, accumulated over the last few years, on man's immediate destiny, notwithstanding the apocalyptic tone which much of it adopts and the divergent (and conflicting) solutions which it proposes. This literature warns of the need to approach the question of a NIEO as part of a fundamental change in the path of development taken by mankind and also by the central societies. The introduction of this viewpoint must enrich the analysis and make it more specific: it must help formulate questions more efficiently. In the first instance it is necessary to understand clearly what is meant by the term New International Economic Order. Does it only mean better prices for raw materials, the industrialization of the Third World, better access to the central markets for the manufactured goods produced in peripheral countries, and economic growth through which social development equal to that of consumer societies will be reached? (This alternative is not necessarily contrary to the interests of the central groups. Moreover it would have the desired effect of a new international division of labor, already in progress, from which certain semiperipheral countries would benefit at the expense of the rest of the Third World and also, naturally, at the expense of the "alternative development" project for mankind.) Or does the reconstruction of the world system imply a redefinition of lifestyles, development patterns, and conditions for the betterment of everyone?

Regardless of the meetings, recommendations, and resolutions of the international forum, the idea of the new order is consistent with fact because it coincides with the movement toward change in the model of accumulation and the international division of labor which is inherent in the model. The discussion about the NIEO cannot, if it is to remain realistic, detach itself from the context of worldwide crisis and transformation, which are intrinsically directed by the interests of the central groups.

The internationalization of productive capital determines the conditions for large-scale reallocation which will certainly promote a partial and distorted growth of some Third World regions. This implies a considerable change from the classic patterns of the international division of labor, but it cannot in any way be considered the end to the search for a more just world system. It is simply a policy of assigning resources in a better way in view of a calculation of private profitability, favored by the presence of transnational companies and the worldwide expansion of the economy. This process has made possible the creation of a world reserve of a potential work force, from which it is possible to choose, according to the criteria of optimum utility. On the other hand, the progress of communication systems and computerization allows organization of the productive process on a world scale without its direction being dependent on geographical location. Finally, the new methods of the production and organization of the work force, through ever increasing specialization, make the rapid training of this work force possible.

This process, which certain authors call the New International Division of Labor,(3) is already in progress and the expansion of these "factories for the world market" is staggering. An estimated global calculation, undertaken by the above-mentioned authors, shows that whereas in the mid-sixties there were hardly any export-oriented industries in the underdeveloped nations, ten years later thousands of factories were operating in no less than 39 developing countries and their products were almost exclusively aimed at the markets of the countries of the central group. This embraces nearly all types of production: textiles, shoe manufacturing, electronics, and a growing tendency to export the products of the steel, shipbuilding, and mechanical industries to the peripheral nations as well.

Naturally, these facts are already well known and the only purpose in citing them again is to update the features of a situation in full process. It is interesting to note that this is the response of transnational capitalism and the advanced countries to the crisis and the demands for the creation of a NIEO. The recognition of the major distribution of power in the world, the persistence of inflation in the central groups, and the scarcity of vital resources act as stimuli to increase the comparative advantage of certain countries in the Third World in producing specific manufactured goods. Undeniably, certain underdeveloped countries will exploit this opportunity in quantitive terms and as a means of expanding their productive strength, the result being that the paths taken by the Third World countries will be increasingly more different. The dilemma is greatest for those semiindustrialized countries in mid-development, such as those in Latin America, which must redefine and readjust their roles within the world market.

If in the end it is this type of New International Economic Order which takes root, the result will be the reclassification of nations within the existing international system. The semiperipherals, having certain advantages within the process of the internationalization of production due to possession of vital natural resources, will rise, whereas the rest will stay in the same position. The staggering growth of the transnational companies has enabled the central groups to collect and transform to their own ends the claims which the Third World started to make over three decades ago. The continuing crisis accentuates this trend, and the successive failures of the North-South dialogue do no more than reinforce the idea that only with true "alternative development" will it be possible to remodel the world order, to close the gap and build a more egalitarian, participative, and democratic world. A utopia? This is, in any case, a more realistic vision than the belief that the NIEO, as we know it, can bring about progress for the peripheral nations.

Let us examine the case of Latin America. A few pages earlier, the Secretary General of ECLA was quoted when he described the path of development taken by Latin America. It seems clear that the region's problems are not due to absence of economic growth but rather to the style of the first stage of this growth in dependent industrial development, which certain authors have called the "internationalization of the market."(4) The elites' attempts to overcome the obstacles to accumulation caused by the "state development" or "national-populist" policies of the 1940-1960 period showed clearly and quickly their socially negative aims, which not only maintained but reinforced the existing inequalities. In 25 years, the average growth rate of the region reached 5.5 percent per annum, a figure which suggests great dynamism, even though if this growth were translated into per capita income, the picture would no longer look so good. In any case, what can be deduced from the analysis of these facts is that in those 25 years, the region underwent an intensive process of transformation, both in the productive system and in the adjustment of its economy to the new characteristics of the world market.

In effect, while in 1950 industry accounted for 17.9 percent of total production, by 1975 the figure had risen to 23.9 percent, while the agricultural and livestock sector fell from 20.1 percent to 13.2 percent. Needless to say, these average figures have relatively greater weight in the larger countries within the region. Social development, however, did not keep up. In 1972, 43 percent of Latin Americans lived in "extreme poverty" and a further 27 percent in "destitution." The 1974-75 recession in the central economies and the attempts at subsequent recovery only worsened the situation, rapidly pushing the potential conflict within Latin American societies to the level of an institutional crisis. Runaway inflation, followed by the subsequent recessionist attempts at controlling it through "orthodox" monetary policies, added serious social and political problems and deterioration to a situation which was unsatisfactory from the outset.

In order to reach a more fundamental and faster adaptation of national economies to the world market and thus allow the chosen style of development to carry on as planned, it would seem that the elites have no choice but to reinforce and speed up the course toward drastic reallocation of incomes within the different social sectors, to the detriment of the most unprotected groups. The immediate result of a policy which aims to retain such unjust structures of domination, inherent in an increasingly concentrative and exclusive form of development, cannot be other than the emergence of new forms of authoritarianism. Thus, the first conclusion is that the maintenance of this pattern of development is incompatible with not only the extension but also the basic existence of democracy.

Tending to adapt themselves to the demands of more open and competitive economies, the current policies of nearly all the large Latin American countries (which try to take advantage of their semiperipheral status) are leading them toward a break in consensus, followed by political crisis and then authoritarianism. They are thus caught in a spiral. The way in which the dominant elites of the countries are adapting to the New International Economic Order, as well as to the New International Division of Labor, is causing a substantial change in the forms of government. This not only prevents them from fulfilling their clearly stated reformist and distributive aims, but in extreme cases it also makes them abandon the liberal-democratic principles of interaction and representation of all interests.

DEMOCRACY AND THE PATTERN OF DEVELOPMENT

The contemporary basic premise is that democracy is the correct political form for a new order, as well as the guiding principle in internal and international relations. On the domestic scale, political democratization appears as a guarantee that economic priorities will be given in relation to social interests. In one of his last essays, Jose Medina Echavarria pointed out:

> The revitalization of the democratic system might be an excellent means of sustaining the continuity of the development process, in particular where the furthering of planning could be achieved by successfully having recourse to the representative forms of government as efficient mechanisms for the mutually consistent implementation of both economic and political options. Or be it the trying out of a political parliamentary system which was also the efficient organ of democratic economic planning, based on the participation of all the parties involved, taking for granted at the outset the existence of their differences and antagonisms.(5)

On an international scale, democracy appears as the prerequisite for a new order. The democratization of relations between nations and the correction of the massive inequality of power between the center and the periphery seem to be the first demands of the Third World movement, which began in the fifties. Therefore, the problem of the New International Economic Order must be seen not only as a problem of international relations, but also as a desire for a fundamental change in the unjust participative structure at all social levels.

It is, however, certain that the problem of democracy in Latin America cannot be raised simply as an abstract discussion. The successive political crises in some of the continent's larger countries give rise to the need for the redefinition of the meaning and aims of democracy as well as the conditions necessary for its establishment. It is a fact that the traditional forms of democracy, linked to the classical Anglo-Saxon model of political liberalism, seem to have entered a stage of exhaustion. The complexity of the conflicts in modern societies requires that the participation of all groups be institutionalized. This institutionalization is not as simple as the theoreticians of the division of power through political parties believed. This fact, indisputable in the case of the more developed countries, emerges even more clearly for the transitional societies which are the victims of a deep crisis of representation. The aims of democratic recovery in Latin America need redefining in relation to the removal of some of the political obstacles which have distorted the establishment of the New International Economic Order. Active democracy should now be on the road toward ever increasing egalitarianism and participative development.

An academic trend with a growing influence in the power spheres of the central countries visualizes, in contrast, that given the characteristics of the present international order, the expansion of democracy has virtually reached its limits.(6) Any increase in participation - that is, any growth toward "fundamental democratization" in Karl Mannheim's sense - would imply sacrifice of other goals, primarily the rational growth of the economy. In the end growth and participation would be essentially contradictory: democracy would already be "ungovernable" and inefficient.

One of the authors of the essay on the crisis of democracy(7) readapted the model in order to analyze political participation in developing countries. The result is the antithesis of the "optimistic equation" which associated economic development with democracy: this "liberal model" of analysis has proved invalid for the peripheral countries. A "benign" model, capable of linking the aims of economic development, political participation, social equality, and stability, is replaced de facto (in the countries of the Third World and still more in the semiindustrialized nations) by two other models which play off each other in vicious circles: the "populist" and "technocratic" models. In a pendular motion, one drops while the other rises in successive historical cycles. The participation and egalitarianism inherent in the populist model serve to erode growth, thus preparing the ground for the technocrat's plan of recovery which will deal with economic development at the expense of participation.

Descriptively, the analysis seems to evoke faithfully the recent history of many Latin American countries, and the vicious circles are closer to reality than the liberal prototype which suggests a linear relationship between development and democracy. However, the plan can be discussed conceptually. It is certain that if the values which support the present patterns of growth are maintained, the extension of democracy will not help development. The problem is that development is not a neutral concept which has only quantitative signs, and only through accumulation qualitative ones. It is not a question of level of development but of its pattern. It is precisely the producer-consumer concept of development and the search for a predatory and exclusive industrial growth which are in crisis in Latin America (and in general in all peripheral countries with a relative level of modernization). To those who affirm the incompatibility of democracy and development, one can reply with a question: what kind of development? This is the point at which the problem of democracy is related to the need to reaffirm its present foundations, insofar as it is only democracy which can be associated with the practical pursuit of a new style of development.

This new pattern is both participative and egalitarian, and therefore the antithesis of the prevailing model which bases itself on technocratic rationale and on the concept of dynamism created for private gain and market laws. In this way the new pattern appears as the basic prerequisite for the creation of a real NIEO.

Thus the relationship is inverted. If at first democracy was conceived as an offshoot of economic growth and it was then realized that this was not necessary, it is possible to turn things around, to determine which type of development favors democracy and which type destroys it.

In his latest works, Raul Presbisch has proposed an exemplary approach to the question. The evolution of peripheral capitalism, he says, "has thwarted two great hopes: that the 'penetration' of the technology of industrial centres would spread its fruits through all levels of society and this would help the advance and consolidation of the democratic process."(8) These hopes can no longer be realized, because the imitative and consumerist capitalism prevalent in Latin America is more and more discriminatory. "The increasing development of the consumer society would appear to become incompatible, in the long run, with the advance of democracy, since it tends to create a growing disparity between the economic and political processes, which is then corrected by repressing the latter rather than transforming the former."(9) In line with the advance of the democratic process, the work force, through its political and trade union power, pressurizes in order to reap part of the fruits of technological progress - which, in the peripheral states, remains largely in the hands of the higher strata, given that the spontaneous, unaided movement of the economy is not sufficient to distribute it to the rest of society. This distributive battle, which brings into question the whole relationship between democracy and the economy, tends to be resolved by sacrificing the former in order to retain economic progress which ensures the continuance of the consumer society.

Democratization is not possible without simultaneous assaults on the problems of accumulation and distribution, that is, without trying to escape from the technocratic and populist vicious circles, which lean in favor of one or other of these directions, thereby leading the political system into a state of chronic instability. However, accumulation and distribution, or the placing of an economic basis for democratization, is unthinkable, according to Presbisch, without changing the system: "There can be no efficient reforms if they are based on the fundamental failures of the system."(10) This is the case if the pattern of development is kept, based on an imitation of the consumer habits of the central groups, which are in turn based on the higher strata securing the benefits of an increased productivity which has been obtained thanks to corporate technical progress. The present predominant course, with regard to the adjustment of the semiperipheral economies to the new international division of labor, tends only to reinforce these distorting trends.

CONCLUSIONS

It is necessary to try to answer a question which has already been presented in the preceding pages: is it possible to attain an equitable order between nations without changing their internal systems?

The course of this argument has been to suppose that a New International Economic Order is a problem of choice between alternatives, that its features will depend on the type of development which both central and peripheral mankind follows in the future, and that this is closely associated with the power structures which prevail in each and every country. The problem, therefore, does not lie only in adopting a strategy in order to eliminate the dissymmetry between nations through constant bargaining in the international forum, but also in looking closely at the domestic level of each society in which an excluding and authoritarian form of development must be eliminated.

Medina Echavarria once pointed out that all the questioning and protest movements of our age are opposed in one way or another to technocratic supremacy and are attempting to achieve participative supremacy in its place. He added that the proposals for a New International Economic

Order cannot avoid the tensions arising from being placed in a continuum, which runs between a "pure example" of participation and a "pure example" of technocracy. Both can be political obstacles to a NIEO and transformations within each country which must accompany it.

Therefore, to avoid falling into extremes, we cannot call the discussions in international fora totally sterile. They are attempts to find different forms of compromise, though, in effect, in the absence of a global discussion on the pattern of development which mankind expects, these dialogues can take on all the appearances of a conversation between the deaf.

In spite of everything, the present situation makes it possible to reanimate the discussion of a NIEO, precisely because there is a growing interdependence between nations and both politics and economics have become more "universalized." Basically, the growing dispersion of world economic power offers a springboard to the claims of some of the peripheral countries, and offers them the prospect of a better deal than the so-called "comparative advantages" they would obtain in the context of a more open world economy.

It is clear that the danger has already been seen. In the current reconstruction, certain semiperipheral countries emerge, privileged at the expense of others, who are attaining certain positions within the partial reclassification, without this altering the global nature of inequality. The worldwide economic changes which support this suggest the difficulties of any attempt to globalize the problems of the periphery. The renegotiations of partial situations by countries or groups of countries, instead of encouraging a direct confrontation between the "club of rich countries" and the "club of poor countries," appear to be the most obvious dodge. An age has ended, and we are going through a transition toward a new stage for mankind. An "alternative" NIEO implies an "alternative" development.

NOTES

(1) "Statement of the Executive Secretary of ECLA, Enrique Inglesias," Latin America; the New Regional and World Scene, ECLA Records, No. 1 (Santiago de Chile, 1975).

(2) Inmanuel Wallerstein, "La crisi del XVII Secolo e il sistema mundiale dell'a economia europea," Studi Storici 2 (1978).

(3) Falker Frobel, Jurgen Heinrich, and Otto Kreye, "The Tendency Towards a New International Division of Labor," Review 1 (1977).

(4) Fernando H. Cordoso and E. Faletto, Dependencia y desarrollo en America Latina (Mexico: Siglo XXI, 1969).

(5) Jose Medina Echavarria, "Apuntes acerca del futuro de las democracias occidentales," *Revista de la CEPAL* 4 (1977).

(6) M. Crozier, Samuel Huntington, and J. Watanuki, *The Crisis of Democracy* (New York: New York University Press, 1975).

(7) Samuel Huntington and J. Nelson, *No Easy Choice* (Cambridge, Mass.: Harvard University Press, 1976).

(8) Raul Prebisch, "Critica del capitalismo periferico," *Revista de la CEPAL*, First Semester, 1976, p. 7.

(9) *Ibid.*, p. 8.

(10) Raul Prebisch, "Planifacion, desarrollo y democracia," *Clasco*, 1978.

4 The Industrialization of Latin America and the New International Economic Order

Jorge Bertini

There is at present a generally widespread conviction that industrial development styles which have characterized the last decades are being redefined; that these processes are underway both in the more advanced nations and in the underdeveloped countries, with their own identity and individual features; and that deliberate action is both indispensable and urgent on international and national levels in order to influence these tendencies.

It is a fact that there have been very profound transformations in the worldwide capitalist economy, with results that are projected at the various levels of international relations and in the implications of national economies.

Structural alterations redefine the basic styles of capitalist development. They have resulted in the nature of the recent crisis, the extension of its manifestations, the persistence of its effects, and the uncertainty concerning the speed and direction of the recuperation process, as well as the expectation that its traces will be strongly projected toward the future.

The fundamental stamp of this accumulation system is an accelerated process of capital internationalization - which is handled by the large transnational corporations - and a gigantic industrial redeployment, which forms new systems in the international division of labor.

Concerning Third World countries, the broad nature of the problems they face implies that any attempt of a sectorial nature would lead to partial and incomplete evaluations. Even so, and without losing sight of this risk, special attention to industrial strategies may be permitted, owing to the frequent identification of industrialization and development, and mainly due to the fact that this is precisely the area that is most sensitive to the effects of transformations in international capitalism. The industrialization pattern followed imposes dominant characteristics on economic and social development, and highly differentiated and important alternative options are outlined against these problems.

Latin America, more so than other Third World areas, has accumulated a certain experience in industrial development. Under present conditions, it has thus had to face fundamental problems and questions about the continuity of this development and its consequences. In Latin America industrialization was identified as an affirmation of national economic independence and as a means of overcoming external imbalances. Likewise the development process was linked with the modernization concept and with the constant absorption of technical progress, with the purpose of raising the material standard of living of the people. It was also intended to convert industrialization into the principal source of employment for the labor force that had been displaced from agriculture.

The expectations have not been confirmed in practice. New systems of dependence, growing contrasts of marginal populations, and substantial differences between the living conditions of some sectors and the extreme poverty of others, constitute symptoms of frustration of those expectations while the gaps between underdeveloped and more advanced countries widen.

From the experience of Latin America it may be concluded that the problems do not lie so much in the pace as in the style or structure of industrialization. In this question the objectives of industrialization are involved. So too is the course of action it must follow, as well as the content of consistent international economic cooperation.

Looked at from this standpoint, there is also the need for a complete and systematic reflection on the course that has been taken in order to identify the indispensable corrections. The undertaking is important, moreover, with regard to other Third World areas that are beginning industrial development. Their thorough knowledge of the Latin American experience would favor a timely definition of industrial development strategies that would help avert critical situations comparable to those to be observed in Latin America.

THE EXHAUSTION OF IMPORT-SUBSTITUTION INDUSTRIALIZATION AND THE NEW WORLD MARKET REQUIREMENTS

The economic course of Latin America in the last few decades now urges the relatively broad acknowledgement of the fact that the pattern for development that took shape with the introduction of import-substitution industrialization has been exhausted. It is undeniable that import-substitution industrialization contributed to greatly modifying regional economic structures: product or median income figures greatly increased, product sectorial structures were considerably altered, populations became predominantly urban, and modernization symbols were widely extended. However, at the same time, there was an accumulation of problems and forces that progressively weakened the process and that finally led to increasingly ostensible tendencies that brought global economic growth to a standstill and exhausted the entire mode of development.

The frustrating image of Latin American development became more accentuated in the early years of the 1970s, notwithstanding the notable acceleration in the growth rate, the significant increase in investment rates, and the reopening of foreign trade sustained by important increases in exports and imports. This generally held view has also been the reason for the growing attention that has been focused on problems in the international economic order and in development strategies, while attempting to identify in them lines of action for self-improvement which respond to what are perceived as external obstacles and internal causes.

The crisis in the international division of labor, based on the specialized exchange of basic and industrial products, had decisive influence on the origin of import-substitution policies. However, notwithstanding its basic orientation of growth toward the domestic market, Latin America was not able to create its own sustained dynamic process for autonomous development. The dependent nature of its economy definitely became more pronounced.

The Latin American economies, basically still dependent on raw material exports, have lost their relative weight in the international market of the majority of the basic products, thus losing bargaining power. On the other hand, with the legacy of dependence based on global processes of international transformation, these economies are called upon to become exporters of industrial products for the markets of powerful industrialized countries.

The tendencies in this direction have already proven to be significantly intensive. In effect, exports of manufactured goods from underdeveloped countries have increased at an extraordinarily fast pace. The annual average rate of increase of these exports went from 12 percent from 1960-66 to 25 percent from 1966-1973, a rhythm comparable to the 17 percent that corresponds to the annual average rate of increase of exports of manufactured goods from developed capitalist nations during the latter period.

Specifically, exports of this type from Latin America increased 23 times from 1955-1974, in contrast to the 11-fold increase for the world in general; and in Latin America,

Brazil, Argentina, and Mexico were most outstanding with annual rates of increase of exported manufactured goods on the order of 34 percent, 23 percent, and 18 percent respectively, from 1960-73.

Hence, the methods and dynamic impulses for industrialization in many underdeveloped countries have varied notably. At one stage, the decisive elements were domestic markets and import-substitution policies. Later, industrial production aimed at placement in the world market was incorporated.

This industrialization model is substantially different from the one which shapes the import-substitution process, where national and international capital seek out domestic markets and in some relatively large unrestricted semiindustrialized economies, it is superimposed. For countries with more reduced domestic markets and limited natural resources, association with the world market via manufactured goods exports may become the dynamic center of their economies, as in the case of Hong Kong or Singapore. However, integration into the world market always tends to be redefined with regard to industrial exporters, in spite of the large existing diversity in their supply of factors, in the distinct degree of scientific and technical development that has been achieved, and their individual national characteristics.

These are the kind of questions that make up programs for negotiating a NIEO with the list of trade, monetary, and financial problems, and the ethics codes that supposedly would regulate transnational activities.

However, the various conceptions of the NEIO are so different that they often become contradictory. For some, it is a question of overcoming the legacy of obstacles to the capital internationalization process; for others, of resisting the subjugation involved in new rhythms and styles of capitalist accumulation on a worldwide scale. While the controversy goes on, a new order is actually imposed which projects very profound consequences on national economies of both capitalist developed countries and underdeveloped countries. Hence, the accomplishments, perspectives, and methods of the process are today topics of compulsory academic and political concern in the triple dimension of their foreseeable effects on capitalist industrialized economies, on economies that are situated at intermediate levels of industrialization, and on those that are defined as relatively less economically developed.

In Latin America the new external conditions are added on to accumulated domestic problems, thereby hastening the exhaustion of the import-substitution model. Thus, the margins for independent national development are drastically narrowed: direct domination is accentuated by increasing penetration of transnational corporations, and indirect domination by the imposition of economic policy plans that worsen the subordinate convergence of Latin American economies to the requirements of powerful capitalist economies.

CONDITIONS AND CONSEQUENCES OF THE INTERNATIONALIZATION OF INDUSTRIAL PRODUCTION

The individual models that are presently adopted by the industrial production process, both in central and peripheral countries, lead to a group of new problems.

The internationalization of production means that a substantial part of the profits, and therefore of accumulation, is sustained by low wages. Reproduction of the system on these bases demands as a necessary condition a job market where labor is cheap and in plentiful supply. Hence, it is important for the corporations that transfer part of their capital to underdeveloped countries to maintain these low salaries. This does not necessarily lead them to prefer countries with absolute low wage scales. The tendency toward equalizing physical labor productivity does imply equipment similar to that of developed capitalist countries and the existence of urban populations capable of adapting to the discipline required for industrial work. In most cases, this requirement is met when there is a margin of urban unemployment that has been created by import-substitution industrialization processes; in other circumstances, manual domestic skills are taken advantage of and reconverted to the requirements of industrial production.

It is not valid to assume that incorporation into the world market of underdeveloped countries by means of exports of manufactured goods constitutes a mechanism for confronting the urgent problem of unemployment and subemployment in these countries. In fact, so great an increase in exports of manufactured products is needed in order to confront this problem that it cancels out the feasibility of the solution. Hence, the question must be asked whether, by means of this new form of integration of underdeveloped countries into the world market, the gap that separates them from developed countries can be narrowed, or if it simply responds to a new pace and style of accumulation by developed capitalist economies that does not affect the situation of underdeveloped economies except in terms of accentuating dependence.

The methods that could definitely bring about the realization of the industrialization process are a matter of conjecture, but the proven facts are sufficient to recognize their importance and even to venture some hypotheses on what their consequences might be. The question is fundamental for Latin America. Problems of efficiency and competitive capacity come to the forefront; protectionist policies and internal price structures are redefined; the criteria for alloting resources and the basic guidelines for accumulation efforts are changed. Among other consequences, all this induces a deterioration of the relative position of lesser productive units that are mainly oriented toward domestic markets, while it favors concentration and export activities.

Internationalization of capital and penetration by transnational corporations qualitatively accentuate and modify dependent relationships by carrying to the extremes the denationalization process of national economies. In underdeveloped countries, the extraordinarily high levels of concentration of production and centralization of capital that are usually obtained quite rapidly, favor the consolidation of some strongly monopolized corporate strata. The reconversion of these exporting economies that is sought leads to a close convergence of these local corporate strata with transnational corporations, while the displacement of domestic markets as the dynamic axis of expansion substantially weakens the position of nonmonopoly entrepreneurs, who are more interested in expanding domestic demand and who contribute independent national development projects within the frameworks of growth schemes that eventually become exhausted.

It is inevitable that the new accumulation and international division of labor systems, in the long run, lead to increasingly more polarized alternatives for internal development: on the one hand, capitalist development guidelines that are wholly subordinate to international capital and that bear a definitely regressive stamp in their social consequences; on the other, the redefinition of an independent national project that places the basic needs of the great majority of their populations at the center of its objectives and as the principle sustaining dynamic process.

In this way, the problems of restructuring worldwide capitalism, from the Latin American perspective, not only deal with the terms of external economic relations, but also very fundamentally with internal development processes and with the outcome of the great social alternatives that are offered in Latin America.

In some cases, these tendencies have been fully imposed. Characteristically, repressive dictatorship regimes sustain projects whose basic economic content specifically seeks this more profound and complete convergence with developed capitalist economies, as well as a restructuring of the productive base which favors sectoral efficiencies at the cost of a concentration of production and centralization of capital, closely associated with foreign capital. The project implies the regression of social advances and the compulsory retention of their demands, so that export possibilities and retribution for the proposed foreign capital increase.

As these governments reach the most difficult stages of the task they have been called to carry out, they offer the possibility for their fortuitous replacement. However, this would always be under terms that do not threaten the permanence of these achievements. This question is at the bottom of the present proposals that advocate a "feasible" or "restricted" democracy.

In other countries, the predominant characteristic is the permanence of regimes that face development problems within the frameworks of a capitalism that must be conciliated with the maintenance and advance of a democratic process and, at times, with efforts at gradually alleviating dependence. It is here that the crisis of the traditional development process is most clearly evident, whereby the sacrifice of social objectives is not accepted - at least not formally - and where its inherent contradictions can be more openly expressed. The problems of foreign economic relations are added to those of internal operations of systems, which are reciprocally nurtured in their interrelations, thereby forming a framework of increasing external imbalances, internal instability and maladjustments, social tensions, progressive loss of dynamic trends, and tendencies toward stagnation.

It is logical that in these last instances transformations in international capitalism are followed with greater concern. A critical and defensive attitude is adopted when the changes make the task of sustaining the system even more arduous and when the risk of regressive influences increases; and a hopeful attitude is taken when the proposals for a New International Economic Order offer different bases for overcoming external imbalances.

The external conditioning factors that are summarized in discussions on the worldwide economic order, and the internal alternatives that are offered as options in the development strategies, bring out some areas of concern that are particularly relevant for Latin American economies with greater relative development. There is the question of the contrast between, on the one hand, relatively greater aptitudes and potential for establishing sustained development and for benefiting from the opportunities of external economic relations, and, on the other, the limitations and inflexibilities accumulated as a result of the course taken within the frameworks of a specific growth and dependence process.

The first instance implies a long history as politically independent nations - the consolidation of a national state that is capable of becoming an efficient promoter of even relatively complex development undertakings, the relative diversification obtained by its productive structure, and the significant representation of the industrial sector in the whole of the product. On the opposing side, there are the features of marked monopolistic concentration, advanced economic denationalization, and exhaustion of relatively easy methods of dynamic growth promotion (substitution of imports of low capital density and few technological requirements, net contributions of foreign debt and foreign capital). The extreme differences in living conditions among different groups occur as a result of an increase in income and the way in which it is distributed, margination of broad sectors of the population, social tensions accentuated by frustrated hopes, and opposing and very diversified interests of social groups that are expressed through relatively powerful organizations which limit the margins for negotiation and compress or divert important amounts of accumulation potential toward unproductive ends. In these economies a productive structure has been defined that narrows down the options and creates highly inflexible situations for substantial reorientations of development purposes. This feature contributes to an increasing loss of effectiveness in the traditional guidelines and tools of economic politics. The lack of a sustained development policy and the periodic alternation of development and stabilizing efforts are seen as factors of uncertainty. This is definitely a kind of double crisis of international insertion and domestic development, which are simultaneous and closely interrelated.

INTERNATIONALIZATION AND DOMESTIC STRATEGIES OF DEVELOPMENT

Domestic development strategies are included within the framework of concerns over the nature and consequences of predominant international economic relations. They are frequently seen as totally independent questions or as purely complementary alternatives and conditioning factors. For some, they are concentrated in the hope for a New International Economic Order that must serve underdeveloped economies as a contribution to overcoming important immediate problems (mainly related to external imbalances) and above all, that will open up new opportunities for dynamic motivation that will not require substantial reorientations of internal methods. For others, however, there are two sides to this same problem. External and internal relations dialectically converge in such a way that a redefinition of internal development strategies would not be feasible if the nature and dynamics of present international economic relations are not substantially modified; likewise, a NIEO would be of little relevance if the very strategy of development is not redefined.

An important step in the concrete design of the meaning and content of new strategic concepts is the identification of certain pressing challenges that have been proposed in the course of Latin American development. In the first place, there is the alternative between a private consumer society and a social consumer society. In other words, the reversion and substitution of certain tendencies, which in fact have become predominant in the conformation of a productive system oriented toward the different demands of high income groups, by others that give priority to the most needed basic products of the population in general. A strategical reorientation that gives priority to the standard of living of the whole population among its objectives for economic growth at least assumes an income distribution far more equitable. At the same time it demands a major alteration of the conformation of the productive structure, which includes reconsidering its sectoral structure in favor of the agricultural sector and of the productive branches of goods and services for general consumption, especially in the industrial sector. It also requires deliberate action for greater convergence of the product to needs of a social nature that do not find their solution in commercial relations: education, health, housing, etc.

Taken separately, neither aspect is new. A better distribution of income and a more rapid increase in food production and other basic consumer goods have always been present in the stated objectives of economic policies, but they have always been included within a system that in fact postpones both of them. The strategic decision would make sense only if they are placed at the center of the objectives for growth and only if the decision takes account of all the factors that it would have to affect so that these transformations could be attained.

The political and economic implications involved in a decision of this nature are obvious. The problems of pace, of the sequence that these requirements should follow, and of the economic feasibility (if the necessary political conditions are present) of very rapid modifications in the appropriation and assignation of the social product, still remain. The maladjustments that this threatens with regard to inherited productive structure demand much more time in order to readjust to new distributive characteristics.

A second important strategical objective necessarily refers to the productive absorption capacity of the labor force. This is a very widespread and rapidly growing problem, which includes requirements for absorbing existing unemployment and subemployment, which emanate from the constant growth of the labor force. The regional experience has shown that this matter cannot be reduced to the problem of the overall rate of growth; nor can it be limited to relative availability of resources - mainly, capital and labor - and policies that can lead to distinct combinations of one or the other in order to favor a greater absorption of labor (for example, through measures that affect their relative prices with regard to capital).

A third question that is necessarily involved in the definitions of a new development strategy involves the terms for insertion of Latin American economies in the world economy. Unless the prospect of a progressive constitution of these economies in entirely subordinate complements of developed economies is accepted, the preservation of the national entity must become another central strategic objective.

The possibility of maintaining the national entity under the spontaneous conditions of the process as they appear cannot be ruled out. On the contrary, a framework of measures would be necessary that would be capable of reverting the denationalization tendencies that have been observed, in order to transform them into a set of factors that are reciprocally reinforced in operative processes directed at recovering and developing a condition of true national economic and political independence. It is surely in the strategic domain that questions on the world economic order and internal development strategies most clearly converge, and in which recent tendencies and the dynamics of international capitalism constitute the main obstacle, above and beyond good intentions and wishes.

One last indispensable element for consideration is situated beyond the strictly economic sphere, although it underlies everything that has been mentioned so far. It is the question of how the visualization of a new development strategy also involves forseeing an essentially participating society, with feasible levels and forms of social participation which are assumed to be indispensable requirements for its own effectiveness.

What is actually happening in the region is more than a search for compatibility between objectives for economic expansion and a democratic development process that are not contradictory to one another. A development strategy based on present conditions, on the extension of the problems, on the scope of the collective effort implied in overcoming them and the introduction of models that are very different from those of the past, could not materialize without an active mobilization of social groups that constitute the majority of the population, which would entail not only their passive support of public objectives, but also transferring to them increasing amounts of direct responsibility at the different levels and modes of expression, and in the direction and administration of the economic process.

BASIC OPTIONS FOR THE FUTURE

If these factors are taken into account and are viewed in the light of the foreseeable evolution of international capitalism and of the fate of the internal economic and social evolution, four basic alternatives could be tentatively proposed for the future paths of industrialization in Latin American countries.

Maintaining Import-Substitution Industrialization

This alternative represents the natural option according to the functioning of Latin American capitalism. A series of accumulated factors and conditions makes its replacement by a progressive model very difficult. For this reason, it will probably continue to characterize the next industrial effort on the part of most Latin American countries.

Regional experience shows the inherent limitations of import-substitution industrialization, even within medium-range perspectives. Its course more or less rapidly exhausts the dynamic phase and leads to persistent tendencies of stagnation and internal and external imbalance. Social tolerance of its consequences progressively diminishes, while it contributes to a growing concentration of income. It involves grave occupational limitations, including the most serious employment problems. Its own dynamics process worsens the dependent condition, facilitates economic denationalization, and creates objective conditions that open the way to other forms of even more regressive industrialization.

Export Industrialization

The basis for an exporting industrialization of underdeveloped countries lies more in the increasing internationalization of capital and production than in internal factors. In the logic of these tendencies, cheap labor in less developed countries constitutes a decisive factor of industrial redeployment by being transferred to activities of stages of processes whose products are basically directed toward markets of developed capitalist countries.

Although the productive orientation of export industrialization is very different from that of import-substitution industrialization, many of the economic and social consequences are similar. It would be very difficult to sustain an industrialization process that would characterize a new historical period of significant duration. This is true not only due to its incapacity for resolving central economic problems of underdeveloped countries (including those of adjusting the balance of payments), but also because of the problems that would result from its extension to more advanced societies: first, with respect to its effects on unemployment levels, and second, with respect to impacts on the real wages of the workers.

An Integrating Industrialization of Underdeveloped Economies

The import-substitution pattern has covered a relatively long period in the historical development of Latin American economies, and since the 1960s export industrialization has been put to the test of practice in various countries. On the other hand, a systematic industrial development effort that jointly commits several underdeveloped countries represents a heretofore untested possibility. Since the 1960s, different guidelines for regional or subregional economic integration have been tested but to a lesser degree and with more limited objectives.

It is very probable that this type of orientation will receive preferential attention and support in the future from international organizations. Its basic content is little more than an enlarged version - on a supranational scale, among underdeveloped countries - of substitute industrialization, which in the end does not alleviate the social imbalances and contradictions inherent in the national phase and as such is not contradictory to sustaining and strengthening the system; therefore it does not conflict with the global interests of the local ruling classes. It is also a type of industrialization that is especially appropriate for apparently technical justifications: the problems appear to be on economic scales insofar as they cover new branches of industrial development and supposedly would be resolved within national markets which, taken separately, are insufficient.

Even so, it still does not appear to constitute an industrialization process for Third World countries capable of predominating during the next historical period. Of course, this is due to the fact that it would still reproduce some of the consequences of substitute industrialization, particularly with regard to problems of employment and foreign dependence; but it is also due to the enormous obstacles for long-term and meaningful comprehension, with their requirements for interdependence and reciprocal concessions among the underdeveloped nations - at times with very great differences in relative development, not to mention the political and cultural differences and their respective relations with powerful capitalist economies. Hence, it is very probable that its effective sphere of operation does not go far beyond the relatively modest limits suggested by regional economic integration experiences that have already been undertaken in the past.

An Industrialization Oriented Toward Basic Needs

Unlike the preceding alternatives, the most important factor here is not global production rhythms or volumes but the objective of equitable industrialization itself. The requirements for the feasibility of the approach exist less in relation to market extensions and are more in keeping with the fundamental objectives of development. In other words, it is an option that involves very profound social transformations, and one of its features includes a very radical progressive redistribution of income and property.

This option demands consistency between the terms that are frequently verbally acknowledged - when it is stated that there cannot be a successful resolution to the problems of international economic relations and of a New International Economic Order without important internal structural transformations - but rarely put into practice. It has also not been sufficiently made clear if these transformations are possible within an increasingly internationalized capitalist system or if they assume the replacement of this system with another.

It is also the alternative that more directly corresponds to the central problems that are generally identified in Third World societies: the great majority of the population existing without access to basic goods and services and without sufficient opportunities for employment and productive and stable jobs.

An industrialization model that centers its objectives on the basic needs of the population assumes the construction of a whole productive apparatus that is a good deal more diversified than a simple listing of its final demands would suggest. The priorities of agriculture and the agroindustry, in response to the urgent need for food, necessarily lead to the development of agricultural machinery and implements industries, and of the chemical industries that supply fertilizers, insecticides, herbicides, and other agricultural inputs. Similar requirements would be made by priority development in other industrial branches, such as textiles, leather, and clothing. Housing priority has direct repercussions on the construction materials industries, and the same thing happens with other objectives that are also transformed into basic needs: infrastructure and production capacity for health, education, and recreation services, each with its own intermediate demands for other types of goods and services that pose needs derived from the expansion of other branches such as the pharmaceutical industry.

It is necessary to develop whole segments of the productive apparatus based on final demands, which are determined by basic needs and in lines that are projected to certain fields of capital goods industries (machinery and equipment, structures, boilermaking, etc.). This implies a kind of industrial headquarters where specific developments in certain areas and relative equilibrium among the different branches of the sector are combined in methods, relations, and proportions very different from those recorded in past industrializing experience. All this must be resolutely promoted - the market cannot do so, or tends to lead these developments in other directions.

Within such a headquarters it would also be possible to identify a range of technological flexibilities that must be taken advantage of based on the general objectives of the model to which it corresponds. Thus, it can also become a very important reference for the definition of scientific and technological policies, as long as the requirements for international efficiency and competitiveness are on a minor scale.

REQUIREMENTS AND CONSEQUENCES OF THE BASIC NEEDS OPTION

The four options do not imply an election proposal. They are not, in fact, alternatives but elements that in reality would be combined in varying degrees. It is precisely the weight each will carry that will define a specific model of industrialization.

In effect, narrow concepts and the image of a categorical opposition between the alternative of basic needs and the elements contained in the other options must be overcome. An analysis must be carried out not only of industrial branches and lines which directly respond to those objectives, but also of necessary intersectorial relations of a global structure of the industrial productive apparatus, relations which should sustain such a structure. Also needed is the projection of this structure's requirements and consequences on other aspects of the social and economic life, including the strategies of scientific research and technological development.

It is not difficult to imagine the importance of a strategy that is inclined toward the formation of an industrial pattern of this type: greater national autonomy, self-reliance, greater absorption capacity for labor in the sector, and possibilities for greater equilibrium in regional development. This is directly complementary to a simultaneous strategy of industrialization aimed at evaluating natural resources, thereby making them the basis for an advantageous position in world market industrial exports, whether it is a question of mineral, energy, agriculture, forest, or marine resources. The total recuperation of those resources is in turn the basis for establishing and controlling the corresponding technological developments, with regard to immediate export and to their valuation in transformation processes undertaken in the country. This valuation would require the concentration of scientific and technical efforts and skills, thereby eliminating the dispersion that has been observed in the region, which is a product of a development model that is oriented toward the immediate requirements of the market.

In this attempt to outline the specific boundaries of an alternative industrial strategy, recognition must be given to other branches of the industrial apparatus that might play a relevant role. They are lines of action that, although they do not necessarily have a strategic character or direct links to basic needs, could assume priority interest insofar as they constitute a basis for joint industrializing efforts in groups of underdeveloped countries. Their role may be very important in regard to problems of complementing and integrating production apparatus which cannot be included in national programs in the face of requirements that are superior in dimension and productive scale in order to reach appropriate levels of efficiency. This leads to the possibility of a joint agreement in which certain lines are programmed for distribution and in which underdeveloped countries achieve important positions in corresponding specialized development, thereby justifying the concentration of scientific and technological development efforts in these countries.

In short, an industrial strategy that is defined on the basis of the basic needs of the population as a central objective can advantageously complement (and in fact, would have to) the elements of the other alternatives that have been described. There is no reason not to retain substitute development processes: this offers a frame of reference for selectively adopting them. It does not sacrifice the potential of manufactured goods exports: instead it orients them toward guidelines that are established on advantageous objective conditions that are different from those of cheap labor, as in the case of the internationalization process. It does not seek or lead to autarchic schema, and it attempts to redefine the terms of its convergence with international economies and offers broad possibilities for cooperation among developing countries.

However, each partial initiative in all of these cases is placed within the framework of a predominant basic model. Therefore, it will tend to adopt courses of action and to project different results from those that have been evidenced in previous experience that was shaped under the preeminence of substitute industrialization.

The most solid elements for an international solution to a global division of labor, cooperation, and a New International Economic Order that support progressive processes and which do not tend to revert them must be based on an innate strategic solution. Paradoxically, it may be affirmed that this type of option in turn represents both the most utopistic and realistic alternative. It is utopistic because it involves far-reaching domestic social transformations. It is realistic because it is increasingly evident that none of the major current problems of underdevelopment will really be overcome if it is not within the framework of these transformations. It is already clear that accumulative social tensions and imbalances cannot be prolonged indefinitely, with their extreme aspects of unequality, injustice, exploitation, and denationalization of our societies.

As regards feasibility, the first thing that would have to be determined is the unavoidable sterility of partial scopes that do not encompass all the problems and the complexity of interrelationships in their diverse manifestations. If the problems actually do originate in the operative dynamics that have been evidenced in prevailing development plans, the truly effective responses must come from development policies capable of creating dynamic global transformation processes.

Adhesion to substitute industrialization - whether owing to a lack of reasonably mature alternative strategies or to a refusal to understand profound transformations - in some cases leads to proposing new phases of industrial development that concentrate efforts in the industries on capital goods. These proposals are even given the rank of new industrial strategies that supposedly would overcome the exhaustion of previous phases and could integrate the industrial sector into a more complete and autonomous structure. So long as these initiatives are redeployed within the basic frameworks of these substitute policies, they may well not represent anything more than another relatively marginal step in import substitution. The general conditioning factors of the model would probably lead to the conclusion that industrial development does not retrieve permanent vigor only because certain capital goods industries are developed, nor does the productive apparatus become more articulate or necessarily acquire more independence or autonomy. Likewise, this does not involve an affirmation of scientific and technological development on its own; it may very well end up being controlled by transnationals or cover production lines that the big capitalist countries are already willing to transfer from their respective technical stadiums.

The same consideration applies to the areas of international economic order and domestic development strategies. Unless they closely converge, these are not independent schemes that offer perspectives for undertaking successful proposals. Denationalization not only deals with foreign conditions, it is also generated within innate development models. A positive change in external conditions, in the absence of internal transformations, would only have transitory effects of alleviating certain problems. In the same way, a reformulation of domestic development strategies would surely encounter insurmountable obstacles if it is not accompanied by significant changes in the makeup of foreign conditions.

Any strategic reformulation in this direction assumes the recuperation of certain effective capacities of global national decision-making, capacities which have notoriously and increasingly diminished owing to the effects of dependence. There appear to be only two alternatives: a sharp break with the traditional bonds of this dependence and a complete reorientation of foreign economic relations, with great difficulties for developed and underdeveloped countries; or the genuine enforcement of international standards that prevent the accumulated results of these dependent relations from diminishing the capacities for national decision-making. This is precisely the meaning of one of the essential points which, from the standpoint of underdeveloped countries, would have to be included in a New International Economic Order.

The changes not only depend on negotiating skills and convincing appeals to international solidarity, but on very powerful economic interests and correlations of forces that are influenced by many factors. It is much less a question of not recognizing the expression of the strategy on a political plane, including the difficulty of acceptance by the powerful countries of development strategies for dependent countries that might not be in harmony with the models that they would like to impose.

Any strategic reformulation implies the capacity to carry out economic policies over and above the resistance and capacity for response of specific groups of innate and foreign interests, notably accentuated in the overall process of monopolistic concentration. The effectiveness of economic policy is given first place along with the need for a critical revision of its traditional formulations and tools. The development of new unconventional means is also fundamental, means which include a substantive reevaluation of the concept and the roles that will be played by the organization and economic direction of public corporations and the various forms of direct state participation.

Based on the present complexities and inherent implications in the proposals for new development and industrialization strategies, economic policy as a system and continuing decision-making process appears to be required in these economies in order to gradually come closer to a planning system. At the same time, it must become the instrument which will facilitate and demand this general social participation.

It is not simply a matter of reproducing in their objectives and methods the attempts at planning that rapidly spread through Latin America during the 1960s. More than adapting the means to central orientations, it is now a question of planning and economic orientation systems that will serve to define other strategies; that is to say, that will constitute an effective means for attending to much greater complexities not only because of problems that have arisen and have become more accentuated since then, but, more than anything else, because of the extraordinary dimensions of the changes that necessarily are involved in the new strategies.

If the urgency and complexity of the changes are great for the developing countries, they are not any less so for developed capitalist countries. If the present process of capitalist accumulation on a world scale and the new international division of labor are going to greatly influence the Third World countries, their consequences will also be very important in their impact on the most popular sectors of the developed capitalist countries. To a certain extent, this compensates for the weakness the underdeveloped countries experience in their demands for progressive transformations of the international economic order until they can find a correspondence with their interests in the social forces within the industrialized countries.

While relationships of domination over the underdeveloped nations evolved within the frameworks of a specialized exchange of industrial products and commodities, and the appropriation of revenues was exercised to a great extent based on the prices of these products, certain contradictions in the powerful capitalist countries could have been alleviated. Under present conditions, the internationalization process brings the weight of the crisis to bear on the popular sectors of the First and Third Worlds.

The struggle for the New International Economic Order is only part of the problem shared by countries and governments. Its comprehension from a social perspective, which involves all the peoples of underdeveloped countries and the workers of the powerful industrialized nations, is just as, or even more, important.

5 Latin American Foreign Trade and the New International Economic Order

Armando Arancibia
Marc Rimez

Among the factors which determine the effects of Latin America's entry into the world economy, the rigidity and difficulties affecting its foreign trade are extremely important. Despite the changes which have taken place over the years in the context of export and import flows, as well as the efforts made to improve the results of international trade, Latin American countries have been unable to find in their trade relations the key to promoting economic growth, and, in the final analysis, to improving the standard of living of the vast majority of their peoples.

The constitution of the United Nations Conference on Trade and Development (UNCTAD) allowed the developing countries to voice their aspirations and put forward arguments for the changing of the principles which inspire the operations of GATT. This has meant that new criteria are being imposed on international trade. They are inimical to the free market norms which are themselves based on an abstract notion of equality which does not take account of the structural differences of the different economies which form part of the world market.

One of the assumptions on which the establishment of a NIEO is based recognizes that the foreign trade of goods and services must be an instrument of prime importance in the motivation of economic development. To release this enormous potential in favor of backward countries, it is proposed that basic reforms be introduced into the present international trade structure, on the assumption that the trade mechanisms now operating reinforce the concentration of wealth in the hands of the industrialized powers.

LATIN AMERICAN FOREIGN TRADE IN THE SEVENTIES

A brief analysis of the features of Latin American foreign trade in the seventies shows that there have been some improvements on traditional trends. However, no substantial changes have been achieved. That is to say, the predominance of primary products in the region's exports has continued. This is reflected in unstable and undynamic income from exports, in real terms.

This thesis is opposed to some of the analyses being made nowadays, where the emphasis is on the diversification of Latin American exports and on their dynamism.

The participation of Latin America in world trade continues to be stagnated, and even more so with the exclusion of Venezuela. In fact, Latin America's percentage share in world exports in present terms continues practically at the same level: 4.2 percent in 1970-72, and 4.3 percent in 1977. Despite an increase in export income, the region has been unable to increase its weight in the international exchange of goods. A similar situation exists for the relative levels of imports which continue somewhat below 5 percent of the world total in 1970-72 and 1977.

The dominant position occupied by commodities in the exports of the majority of Latin American countries, as well as the region as a whole, is a feature which has not changed much over the years. In fact, for several countries the proportion has increased over the last decade, due to the effect of price changes (for example coffee in Colombia), or due to the substitution of goods. The probable future development of Mexico's export sector is a case in point, given the growing importance of the oil sector, after its exports of manufactured goods had reached over 40 percent of total exports in 1974. Even Brazil, whose manufactured goods sales today appear the strongest and most dynamic of the region, obtains nearly 60 percent of its income from the export of commodities.

Commodity prices have continued to be highly unstable. To estimate the extent of this phenomenon we can take the variation coefficient, the variance divided by the mean. Calculated on annual averages, for seven of the ten major agricultural products and for three of the four major minerals (excluding oil) the figure is higher for 1970-77 than for the period between 1963 and 1970. Furthermore, several products were affected by quite substantial price drops in real terms, as was the case with bananas, meat, and copper, among the worst instances for Latin America.

Although it is true that some diversification has taken place in Latin American exports in the present decade, especially through the expansion and dynamism of the manuufacturing sector, it seems appropriate that we should examine the real extent and meaning of this change.

According to the Economic Commission for Latin America (ECLA), sales of industrial goods made in Latin America and sold outside had increased from 13.2 percent of the total volume of real exports in 1970-72, to 23.4 percent in 1975. Despite the fact that this increase of 75 percent in five years can hardly be considered unimportant, it is still not enough to mean a qualitative radical change in the structure of regional exports. The same figures show that the incidence of primary commodities was reduced only from 86.8 percent to 76.6 percent in this same period.

ECLA includes in its calculations of manufactured exports those products which are the result of assembly operations. It is difficult to consider goods assembled in the region as manufactured exports, since we are dealing with processes which are quite unconnected with the rest of the local system of production: they are confined to the application of cheap labor to the finished product.(1)

In Mexico, where assembled goods make up an important and growing source of income ($500 million in 1977, representing 36 percent of the export of manufactured goods in the strict sense of the term, and 26 percent according to ECLA's definition), their operations are accounted for in the balance of payments under the figures for services rather than under those for exports.

Furthermore, ECLA talks of "real exports." Calculated according to present values, the export of manufactured goods comprised just under 18 percent of the volume of exports in 1975. We still have to deduct from this figure the value of assembled products, which can be estimated at about $600 million, that is, almost two percent of the total. Hence we can argue that, even if the position of manufactured goods in Latin American export figures increased, this change of only three percent does not allow us to claim any substantial structural transformation. The fact, therefore, that in Haiti, for example, the export of manufactured goods (CUCI 5-8) accounted for 40 percent of the total value of exports in the fiscal year 1975-76(2) does not mean that a more stable combination of exports has been achieved. On the contrary, given capital's mobility to take advantage of the changes in salary differences and to adapt to a modification in the sociopolitical climate,(3) in terms of industrial assembly activities, the variable nature of Haiti's export income is reinforced.

Apart from methodological considerations it is not possible to evade questions relating to the continuance and extent of growth and dynamism of manufactured goods exports. In the cases of countries like Chile(4) and Uruguay, the increase in nontraditional exports, in general, and of manufactured goods, in particular, is directly linked to the drastic cutting down of domestic demand and the change in direction which these countries are attempting to impose on the system of production, by means of stabilization policies and the liberalization of foreign trade. In Peru, expansion is sustained by means of subsidies and export incentives, which although established as a temporary expedient, could well be transformed into permanent measures. Nevertheless, we can foresee that a recurrence of internal demand would impose the necessity of redirecting at least a part of manufactured goods now exported.

It is not easy to imagine indefinite growth in the export of manufactured goods, given the very nature of the products involved. The types of industry now being developed in Latin America are concentrated more in traditional goods, such as textiles, footwear, leather and wool, and basic steel products, among others. We are dealing with industries, subject to a definite process of internationalization and relocation, which have lost their dynamism and leading role in economic development. They do have features in common with primary commodities, among which is their low income-elasticity of demand. Such industries are exposed to fierce international competition and the existence of overproduction at a world level, which in turn are reflected in considerable price drops in the market; this leads to an increase in protectionist trends in industrial countries.

Even the location of manufacturing plants of dynamic industries in the periphery offers limited prospects. An example of this can be seen in the production of the Volkswagen car in Brazil, Mexico, and Nigeria where a model is produced which Europe now considers obsolete and which has been replaced by technologically more advanced vehicles. Naturally, these countries showed a substantial increase in their exports of transport equipment in the world market. However, as the demand for the models they produce tends to decrease, at least in the developed countries, it seems obvious that it will not be possible to sustain the same exceptionally high growth rates.

The different factors we have mentioned tend to show how relative is the significance of manufactured goods exports and the capacity of such exports to modify the structure of regional sales abroad in any substantial way. We must add the more dynamic role played by transnational corporations in the field of manufactured goods exports, despite the fact that their activities appear to be fundamentally linked to domestic markets. Although we shall consider this point later in the paper, it is useful to stress that the export activity undertaken by such firms is in line with their strategy on a worldwide scale, rather than linked to the needs of the countries on the periphery in which they operate.

Last, intraregional trade has remained relatively stable and has not been established as an outstanding factor sustaining the expansion of Latin American exports. Trade between members of the Latin American Free Trade Association (LAFTA) countries rose from 10.8 percent of the total volume of exchanges in 1970-72 to 13.5 percent in 1976, while transactions between all the countries of "Developing America" were 19.7 percent of the total in 1976 compared with 18.3 percent in 1970-72. At the same time these figures show that the projects of integration considered by different countries in Latin America did not have the expected results, even in matters of trade.

EVALUATION OF OFFICIAL STRATEGIES

The above outline of trends in Latin American foreign trade in the seventies gives a brief picture of the limited effects achieved by the strategies put forward or agreed upon by the United Nations in order to attain a New International Economic Order. In fact, there has been no success in achieving either a stabilization of income, a substantial and lasting diversification of exports, or any sustained increase in the price of primary commodities.

Generalized System of Preferences

The idea of a Generalized System of Preferences (GSP) to obtain free and preferential access to the markets of the developed countries, which would be nondiscriminatory and nonreciprocal, was put forward in 1964 by the Group of 77 and rejected by the United States in UNCTAD I. Later, during UNCTAD II, the proposal was accepted "in principle" and has taken shape, in a very limited way, over the seventies.

The system is in no way "generalized," since it is subject to a whole series of restrictions and conditions. With a few qualified exceptions, raw materials are excluded; some manufactured products remain outside the profit zone or are subject to quota limitations or maximum values; and, finally, the system has been set up for a period of ten years only. Besides, the U.S. Trade Law requires underdeveloped countries to fulfill certain conditions before they can take advantage of the preferences. The outstanding condition is that they do not belong to a producer association - which would violate the Charter of Economic Rights and Duties of States. On the other hand, frameworks of special preferences have been introduced by means of particular agreements, bilateral or multilateral, such as the Lome Convention.

It would surely be of interest if some specialized organization were to analyze the real benefits for developing countries in general, and Latin American countries in particular, to be derived from their exports of manufactured and semimanufactured goods. Available estimates suggest that the effects of the system are minor. In 1976 only 12.3 percent of exports from Latin America to the United States were on the list of goods which could take advantage of the system. However, once the different restrictions had taken their toll, only 7.6 percent of the total could actually benefit from the preferences. Similarly, it has been calculated that if Latin America made full use of the preferences established by the European Economic Community (EEC), annual exports to the region would increase by 0.11 percent annually. This figure, if all underdeveloped countries are taken into consideration, would increase to 0.17 percent per annum.(5)

Factors which explain the low effectiveness of the preference system include the limitations established for the concession of preferences with respect to "sensitive" products; the safeguarding clauses which suspend the application of immunities when an industry faces adverse conditions; lack of flexibility in the regulations on the country of origin, in that only the aggregate value of one country is considered, and not that of different developing countries which might be part of an integrated regional framework; the differences and complexities of administrative systems designed by various developed countries to take advantage of the preferential framework; and the need to allow margins of special privileges to regions or nations linked in particular ways to the central powers.

A high proportion of Latin American exports fall within the category of "sensitive" or "semisensitive" products, which are therefore also affected by the restrictions imposed on processed agricultural products. (The importance of the conditions is confirmed by the recent announcement that Latin America is due to suffer the loss of preferences on 139 articles it exports to the United States, by virtue of the clause on "limitations on the needs of competition" established by the Trade Law. It must be pointed out that of the goods on the list, 127 went over the limits in the first months of 1978 and the other 12 were just about to go over in October of the same year. Fifteen countries will be affected.)

The progressive lowering of tariffs, agreed at different rounds of negotiations - Dillon, Kennedy, and Tokyo - is aimed fundamentally at resolving the trade problems between developed countries, and has only favored exports from backward countries by reflex action, and then only marginally. The tariff structure of the developed countries still retains one essential feature, namely that protection levels are on the increase as the level of product processing increases. Furthermore, due to forces demanding the defense of domestic economic activities, such as the agricultural sector, high tariffs are maintained on primary products and goods, resulting from different stages of later production of special interest to Latin America, as they are among the best placed for producing such goods for the international market.

The methods adopted and the orientation followed in the establishment of the GSP are fundamentally linked to the preoccupation of companies in developed countries with fragmenting their system of production and moving labor-intensive stages out to the periphery. In order to facilitate subcontracting for the transnational companies, measures are taken to freely allow in goods which have been partially manufactured abroad. Thus, for example, the United States set out regulations whereby calculations had to be made in relation to the value added abroad, and not in relation to the total value of the product, with no limitation of physical volume or value.

The recognition of problems found in the operation of the system and the extent of the tariff preferences does not imply a rejection of any attempt to obtain corrections and improvements which might be of interest to the region. The issue is that the developed countries have not been willing to put them into practice, despite the fact that the preferences are not a serious threat to their economies. We need only recall that according to the United States Tariffs Commission, "in general, the tariff preferences allowed by the United States to developing countries will not greatly affect the American economy."(6)

Exports from the periphery also face a great variety of nontariff barriers. These have tended to increase over the last few years, thus cancelling out any progress which might have been made in the field of tariffs themselves. These restrictions are imposed both on primary products and manufactured goods, many of these being what developing countries find easiest to supply. To these are added the limitations "negotiated" bilaterally with the main suppliers, such as those connected with the steel industry.

A substantial improvement in the possibilities of access to the markets of the industrial countries for the exports of developing countries seems unlikely, particularly in a framework of intensification and reinforcement of protectionism. Even GATT had to recognize that "in 1977 import restrictions imposed by the industrialized countries rose considerably, the majority being applied to certain well-defined sectors," and that "as a consequence of this and of previous events, there are now more restrictions on world trade than five years ago."(7)

International Agreements on Commodities.

This is one of the instruments around which there is a wide body of experience in the international field. The first agreements were signed before World War II, and in the period following, under the new criteria established by the Charter of Havana, efforts were intensified to sign agreements between the producers and consumers of basic commodities. However, the results of this effort have been somewhat disappointing for the developing countries and particularly for Latin America. Agreements achieved (olive oil, sugar, cocoa, coffee, tin, and wheat) were the result of a lengthy and protracted process and their lack of effectiveness does not promise much for the negotiations now taking place on natural rubber, although they are part of the Integrated Commodity Programme. The Sugar and Wheat Agreements continue to exist as merely administrative organizations concerned with the study and exchange of information with no real economic effects. The limitations faced by the International Coffee Organization were reflected in the protracted and difficult negotiations over the agreement of regulations on the fixing of prices in a period which saw high quotations on the international market and delay in the setting up of agreed upon reserves. The inefficiency of the stabilization system designed by the present Cocoa Agreement and the resultant discrepancies over renegotiations terms raise doubts about its future once the present agreement expires in September 1979, when a new document has to be signed. The International Tin Agreement has operated better, but recently witnessed serious differences among its members when an increase in the maximum price was proposed, due to the fact that for months it had been well below the price quoted on the market.

In many cases the major producers and consumers have opted not to join the agreements in order to retain freedom of action. There is serious conflict over appropriate methods of determining prices, but also over issues of decision-making and the solution of differences which arise in the interpretation and implementation of different rules and regulations.

In the background lie different perceptions of the objectives of agreements. With very few exceptions, for the developed countries it is a matter of obtaining guaranteed access to commodities under stable price conditions. But, in any case, proposals to prevent violent price fluctuations and to stabilize export income have not been fulfilled in the short term in any substantial way.

The survival of existing agreements seems to be based on the difficulties and obstacles to progressing to alternatives which would be more suitable and effective. Developing countries are increasingly skeptical about this system of negotiating product by product, and stress the need to find a means of tackling the problem of marketing basic commodities in an integrated way.

The Integrated Programme for Commodities

Adopted by means of Resolution 93 at UNCTAD (Nairobi, May 1976), this program has a multiple focus and refers to a wide range of basic commodities including, in an integrated way, different kinds of measures. This concept is not new. At the end of UNCTAD I, there was a recommendation to negotiate agreements on groups of products. Some of the measures, similarly, had been proposed or implemented before. But they now form part of a global scheme which attempts to bring new proposals and modes of operation into the agreements, such as to increase the level of transformation of goods in exporting countries and improve their competitiveness with synthetic and substitute products.

The approval of the project raised hopes and the initiative was seen as a launching of efforts to lay the basis for a new order. However, progress until now has not been promising. It has only been possible to start tentative negotiations on an international agreement regarding natural rubber, while work on other products has not yet gotten beyond the stage of preliminary discussions, apart from that which is already the substance of existing agreements. The setting up of regulatory reserves is a priority and is in fact the key to the whole plan; this accounts for the creation of a Common Fund to finance it. The increase in resources needed to form the stocks of the 18 commodities included in the Integrated Programme for Commodities is estimated at some $6 billion, of which some $3 billion would be needed to set up the fund. It was also calculated that an approximate additional 3 percent of the cost of acquiring the reserves would be needed to cover storage costs.

Although the idea of the Common Fund was accepted in principle, the same acceptance was not given the principles on which the Fund was to be organized. The projects put forward, in the course of negotiations, by developing and developed countries differ substantially in respect to underlying concepts, financing, and the extent of initiative. Although it is true that the conference held in Geneva in November 1978 led the way to new lines of thinking, it is also true that the two blocs were not able to come together and the idea has still not materialized. The problem of finance remains one of the points of divergence since the developed countries (group B) are unwilling to go over $200 million as a first contribution, while the developing countries (group A) need no less than $500 million to finance their stabilization reserves.

Similarly, for the "second window" aimed at other measures - increase in productivity, research and development, support for diversification - the industrialized countries suggested $200 million as a voluntary contribution while the developing countries demanded a compulsory contribution of $300 million. There are also differences over the definition of the scope of the "second window."

The possibility of finding alternative sources of finance has been explored, with the collaboration of the oil-exporting countries. There are precedents in Latin America, such as the agreements signed by Venezuela with Peru and some Central American countries, in the latest attempt to support the policy of retaining coffee exports. For its part, OPEC, through the Director General of its Special Fund, announced to the Conference on the Common Fund that it was prepared to make a contribution to the financing of the stabilization of raw materials, although the Director General did not give a precise figure.

Help from this source could be decisive in setting up the fund. According to some estimates, OPEC will receive in 1979 some $4.5 billion under the heading of the 14.5 percent increase in the price of oil alone. Furthermore, advantages would be gained by no longer having to depend on the attitudes of the developed countries for the implementation of the initiative and the ensuing administration of resources, while at the same time the negotiating powers of the producers would be reinforced.

Producer Associations

This instrument of collective defense of the interests of developing countries in the production and marketing of basic commodities can be characterized as one of the first expressions of concern of the periphery to introduce changes in their international economic relations. Although these expressions preceded the proposal for a NIEO, they made a major contribution in the maturing process of that initiative. Export associations are one of the consequences of the disappearance of that view of the world which saw only the functioning of the market and free exchange as capable of bringing growing benefits to all nations.(8)

The first association, OPEC, was born in 1960. In the same year the Inter-African Coffee Organization was formed, and subsequently the Alliance of Cocoa Producers (1962), the African Corn Council (1964), the Intergovernmental Council of Copper Exporting Countries (1967), and the Asian and Pacific Coconut Community (1969), to be followed by the associations of natural rubber and pepper producers. Behind the rise of such organizations lay the tendency of prices of the respective products to fall with consequent imbalances in the foreign sector of exporting countries, together with the refusal by some of the most important consumers to take part in international agreements drawn up to deal with problems of commodity exchange.

At the beginning, when there was relative economic dynamism and expansion of trade, the association kept to action of a mainly defensive nature: market research, requests for information from producing firms, research into possible new ways of using commodities, exchange of scientific and technical information on production and marketing, and solidarity among members.

In the first years of the present decade the crisis of the monetary system, inflation, and international conflicts encouraged the nations on the periphery to adopt a more active and extensive pursuit of their own interests. The success of OPEC in fixing the price of oil and demanding higher prices, the improvement in the price of other basic commodities, and the increasing demands for a NIEO all encouraged the setting up of new producer associations, of which there are now 20. Among those which are of special significance to the region are the International Bauxite Association (IBA), the Union of Banana Exporting Countries (UBEC), and the Economic Group of Latin American and Caribbean Sugar Exporting Countries (EGLACSEC), all set up in 1974, the last two being formed exclusively of Latin American countries. At the same time there was an increase in the membership of existing groups.

These associations have taken a more decisive role in the market with the purpose of obtaining fairer and more remunerative prices for their products. It is also true that their aims go far beyond those of a cartel: they propose organizing international reserves and coordinating national stocks and, in general, acting as instruments of finance, reciprocal information, solidarity, production diversification, research and development, and personnel training and development.

Except for a few noted exceptions, we are dealing with organizations made up exclusively of nations on the periphery (the industrialized countries have no role to play in them), and this is conducive to a unification of interests and action. Experience shows that we are dealing with one of the instruments which developing countries can use to great effect in increasing their negotiating strength.

The power to form an association in order to intervene in the market, as well as the particular form of the organization and its operation, depends on the nature and characteristic of the product itself: whether it is mining or agricultural, the degree of manufacturing involved, methods of marketing, the structure of world supply and demand, the existence of transnational companies, etc. In short, the negotiating strength of an association is a function of economic as well as technological and political factors.(9)

OPEC is an extreme case, since it is in a position to control the market and fix prices unilaterally. Not all products have the same characteristics as oil. Perhaps the most explicit - and crude - picture of the fundamental elements which must exist before one can judge the negotiating strength of a producer association is to be found in the special report prepared for the United States Congress on the use of food resources in the aims of diplomacy:

> For a country to be able to exercise power over food resources, based on the control of a particular market, four conditions must exist simultaneously. These are: 1. - The importing country must require large quantities of the product; 2. - The quantity required must be a significant proportion of total domestic consumption; 3. - The non-existence of other available sources or ones able to be rapidly developed, other than in the country which intends to use the power of food; and 4. - Lack of satisfactory substitutes in adequate quantities which could be obtained from other sources. If any of these conditions is lacking, the only effect of the United States' refusal to export the foodstuff to the country concerned would be to force it to turn to other sources to fulfill its needs and/or reduce its consumption.(10)

The study refers to foodstuffs but its conclusions can be extended to more or less all basic commodities.

The strength of an organization depends on its members controlling a considerable proportion of production, exports, and reserves; demand must be inelastic in relation to international prices; it is better if membership is not too great in number, in order that members have the closest possible political affinities and that production costs do not vary too much among them; and members must have at their disposal effective means of influencing prices and sharing the market among themselves.

The Latin American experience in this field is varied. Two countries in the region - Ecuador and Venezuela - are members of OPEC, and their success is well known. All that has to be added to what has already been said on pricing policy is that their members have used other means to increase their domestic share of the profits of the industry, such as the nationalization of extractive processes and the increase in the products' transport fleet.

Another association directly linked to the interests of the areas is the Intergovernmental Council of Copper Exporting Countries. It has achieved control of 72 percent of world copper exports, but only produces 46 percent of the output of countries with market economies; on the other hand, it is a market which is highly sensitive to variations in the level of industrial economies where the incidence of imported supplies is not very high.(11) Thus, the organization's influence on the price of the metal has been limited, despite attempts made to restrict production and exports.

Despite its fairly recent creation, the International Bauxite Association is in a better position. Seventy-five percent of bauxite exports in the Western market passes through its hands and consumers are basically dependent on the imported mineral. Ninety-six percent of the bauxite consumed in the United States comes from abroad, and in particular from the Caribbean. Another advantage of the industry is that the proportional price of the mineral in the total production costs of aluminium is low, which enables any rise in the raw material prices to be easily absorbed. With the intention of increasing their share in aggregate value, the producer countries such as Guyana have been taking a line of nationalizing deposits, or, as in the case of Jamaica, relating export taxes to the price of finished aluminium ingots. However, the organization's strength is affected by the existing substitutes for aluminium, as well as the possibility that, in the longer term, technological developments will enable aluminium to be obtained from products other than bauxite.

The Union of Banana Exporting Countries is hampered by a much more complex set of problems. First, its membership comprises countries producing only 45 percent of world banana exports, due to the absence of the major supplier - Ecuador, which produces 20 percent - and of other producers. Second, and worse, only three transnational corporations control the production, marketing and transport, insurance, and other activities connected with the supply of the fruit. The situation is such that for each dollar's worth of banana supplied to the consumer, only 11.5 cents are received by the producers. To deal with this, the members of the association agreed to adopt jointly certain tax measures, so that if it were at all possible to intervene to raise the price, the banana firms would reap the benefit. But this initiative was resisted and after "serious confrontations with the multinationals lasting from April to October 1974...the initial tax of $1 per case was lowered to between 25 and 35 cents per case. This tax is now held at between 40 and 45 cents per case."(12) The organization also created the Multinational Banana Marketing Board (COMUBANA) to make inroads into the distribution process.

There seems to be no justification for the arguments on which the hostility of the developed countries are based, to the effect that excessive power is concentrated in these organizations, susceptible of being used in an arbitrary fashion. In fact, the organizations have a scope of action which they cannot surpass without acting against the interests of their own members. Thus, a considerable increase in the price of a basic commodity might make it profitable to start the process of marginal production or the use of substitutes, as well as raising the price of the manufactured goods they are used for.

All in all, the setting up of producer associations improves the position of member countries, although the impact on product prices has been little, and the great potential of the instrument cannot be used to the full in practice. Their existence increases the power to make decisions which improve the marketing of goods (standardization of contracts; uniformity of technical specifications; presentation and processes), or which increase the countries' share of the surplus generated from the exploitation of resources (export taxes, the demand for more product processing to take place inside the country, the creation of multinational companies to share in the transport and distribution of the products, and even the recovery of property in productive activities). Without being the optimal solution, these producer associations have proven to be one of the most effective mechanisms for developing countries to defend their interests.

Share in Invisible World Trade

Progress in international cooperation between the industrial and developing countries has not been of any significance in this field either. As far as transport is concerned, the situation in Latin America has not changed much despite the fact that transport capacity, especially maritime, has increased in absolute terms. The outstanding example in the region is Brazil, whose policy has been to expand her fleet. But the Latin American share of world tonnage is below 3 percent, which explains its limited influence in this activity.

Freight charges have tended to rise persistently over the last few years, with a corresponding impact on exports from this area. This is where the concern over the operations of shipping conferences stems from, since they quite arbitrarily fix freight charges and terms of transport. The Convention on the Code of Conduct of the Shipping Conferences, notwithstanding its importance in reaching a better balance of interests between the suppliers and users of regular shipping line services, has still not fulfilled the conditions necessary for its application. Besides, some countries in Latin America have less need than others to apply this test, given that their lines have been included in the conferences as ordinary members.

The best way forward is through action which depends on the efforts of the developing countries themselves to cooperate, especially in Latin America. Despite delays and difficulties, ECLA has shown a readiness to work out a maritime transport policy on a regional basis. This has already borne fruit in the guise of the Water Transport Convention, which has confronted the problems associated with the distribution of freight. Along with this, several countries are encouraging the development of their navies through bilateral agreements, which reserve for ships carrying the signatories' flag the transport of all or part of their mutual exchanges. Other nations are adopting measures making it compulsory to transfer a significant proportion of their foreign trade to their own national shipping companies. Last, the creation of the Caribbean Multinational Shipping Company (NAMUCAR), initially made up of six countries, constitutes an important step in taking advantage of the possibilities offered by the pooling of resources and collaboration between the countries of Latin America in order to attempt to solve common problems. This multinational corporation helps to eliminate dependence in matters of transport and encourages trading and exchange inside the area itself, since it extends routes to ports which the larger transnational shipping companies had no interest in reaching. In this way, they avoid the forced mediation of the latter in relations between countries which are geographically very close. There is, however, much ground still to be covered, on a regional level and in relation to the underdeveloped world as a whole.

The development of land transport opens similar opportunities for the broadening and deepening of exchange and communication in Latin America not only in economic matters, but in social and cultural terms.

A similar situation exists in the field of insurance and related services such as banking and credit facilities. The insurance market, and, most importantly, reinsurance, is heavily controlled by companies located in the countries of the center, by direct means or through links with local companies. Although some measures have been adopted both at a national level (the setting up of insurance companies) and at a regional level (for example, the Latin American Reinsurance Pool), this continues to be an important source of loss of foreign currency.

It can be concluded that it has not been possible to achieve an effective increase in the region's share of trade in "invisibles" and that progress has been very slight in the organization of efforts among the countries on the periphery, despite the alternatives opened to them to improve their situation in this field in some way.

OBSTACLES TO A NEW ORDER IN INTERNATIONAL TRADE

Efforts aimed at attenuating the huge and growing gaps within the international community have until now come up against serious obstacles which have delayed the introduction of the changes considered to be indispensable to the establishment of an economic order based on principles of justice, equity, and effective equality in the relations between member countries.

Over the last decade different factors appeared to lend substance to the hope that the so-called Third World might be transformed. The breaking up of almost all of the old colonial systems; the development of information and communication systems to allow developing countries to improve their relative position in this field; the weakening of the absolute hegemony of the United States in the economic sphere and the emergence of new powers such as Japan, Federal Germany, and other European countries; the policy of detente, which reduces the risks of open confrontation; the expectations of the industrialized nations to increase their presence in the rest of the world; and the growing importance of raw materials, foodstuffs, and renewable resources in general, as well as manpower, for the functioning of the central economies, were, among others, phenomena which encouraged the periphery to be more decisive in putting forward their demands.

However, there has been no significant progress; on the contrary, there is a growing feeling of discouragement and failure in certain areas. Many of the formulations and initiatives, such as the Declaration and Programme of Action on the New International Economic Order or the Integrated Programme for Commodities, are too recent for their results to be evaluated, but we must also recognize that awareness of the problems and the search for solutions to them are not new issues to the international arena nor to specialized organizations. In fact we are talking about a movement whose first steps were taken at Bandung, and which was revitalized by the action of the Group of 77 in the framework of UNCTAD.

It is interesting to explore the reasons behind the relative failure of the majority of the proposals intended to change the structure of the international economic system, as well as the adoption of urgent measures to tackle particularly pressing problems. Of special interest for the purposes of this paper is an investigation into the difficulties encountered by innovations in the field of international trade, from the Latin American viewpoint.

The Concept of a New International Economic Order

The first question centers around different members' understanding of a NIEO. The developing countries have managed to organize themselves in reference to a set of proposals and initiatives, contained in a number of studies and reports, and brought together in several United Nations resolutions. Nevertheless, it is difficult to see objectives fully and integrally shared by all the countries on the periphery, which adds to the difficulty of going forward with precise and clear definitions on the means of achieving objectives. Behind the possibilities of imagining a finished common platform lies the assumption that the Third World is homogeneous and there is an identity of interest among its members; this assumption also needs close examination. On the other hand, the central powers of the system do not share the vision which demands the introduction of basic changes in the international set-up, nor do they share the fundamental aspirations put forward by the poor nations. This fact took on special significance during the celebration of the Conference of International Economic Cooperation, in which no one specified the content of the new order.

The vast literature on the problems of the current world economic order and its possible future course opens up a wide range of alternative solutions. To identify them, three concepts are generally used.

At one extreme there is the view that attributes the present conflict to the existence of deeply routed structural imbalances, which subject developing countries to a situation of dependence and exploitation by developed countries. According to this version, the new order can only be achieved through the total transformation of the present system, giving the Third World countries their long denied opportunity to take advantage of the same development possibilities as the industrialized countries, thus ending their situation of dependency. It also requires a new and substantially different long-term development strategy.

At the other extreme we see the "conservative" position, which rejects outright the idea of a new order as unrealistic and impractical, but calls for concessions to the developing countries to satisfy their most urgent demands. According to this view, the present order should be gradually improved by means of a process of introducing marginal adjustments to solve particular problems as they occur.

Between both extremes lies the "moderate position," which puts forward the need for the introduction of basic corrections in the structure of the economic relations between countries, in order to establish a new, just, and reasonable international order which will allow the developing countries to make more rapid progress, and close the distance separating them from the rich countries. This concept rests on the recognition of a growing interdependence between the different elements of the international community, in which development and underdevelopment must be recognized as integral parts of one and the same process. It is necessary, therefore, to reach an agreement which will allow the imbalances between participants to be corrected on the basis of principles of equal rights and mutual convenience. By virtue of this, the developed countries' access to the energy sources and raw materials of the periphery should be compensated for by the latter's access to the markets, capital, and technology of the industrialized world. In this way, the new order would allow developing countries to take a fairer share in world income and make a significant intervention in international institutions.

With logical variations and subtle differences, and beyond the rhetoric used in its formulation, proposals concerning a NIEO can be more or less described within any of the main trends mentioned. Certainly such differences of opinion make it difficult to reach an understanding and move toward the building of a new order. It is also obvious that such differences of focus do not correspond to arbitrary interpretations of international problems, nor to purely dogmatic or theoretical differences. Behind the conflicting visions lies, in the last analysis, the diversity of interests and situations of the members of the world system.

International Transfer of Resources and Internal Transformation

The different interpretations of the concept of the NIEO reinforce the need to define some of the most outstanding features of such an order, according to the aspirations of the great mass of people living in the poorer parts of the world.

First, it is not possible to reduce the problem to the simple improvement and stability of basic commodity prices, to the relatively freer access to the markets of the center, and to a greater degree of industrialization, despite the immediate importance of these objectives. They do not themselves necessarily conflict with the interests and perspectives of the metropolis. They can even coincide with the views of the world economy where the inequalities existing today are not greatly changed. The statements made in international fora show that the aim of the developing countries is to use the present trends of the world economy as a means of reducing the gap which separates them from the rich countries. This aspiration inevitably implies some transfer of resources in favor of the former, through a set of channels and measures. The crucial aim, therefore, is to build a new set of institutions and change their structures in terms that allow the periphery a significant increase in its influence on international affairs and its share in the benefits of economic links, as a means of accelerating its development.

Second, the reformulation of the present order should not be restricted to the international environment. It should also be extended to the domestic situations of the underdeveloped countries. However, this dimension remains on the level of declamatory statements, a fact which is understandable since we are dealing with matters affecting the sovereignty of each country. All in all, if no progress is made in this direction, despite all eventual achievements in foreign economic relations, it will not be possible to see the emergence of an equitable economic order.

Latin America is a good example of this problem. Despite its undeniable economic growth over the period since World War II, the great majority of its people remain in a situation of poverty and backwardness, due to the concentrated and exclusive pattern of the development process of societies in the region.

The developed countries have discovered in this a motive to justify their reticence in the face of demands to redefine their relations with the Third World. They insist that the progress of the developing countries is essentially a function of their domestic economies and the responsibility for them lies with national governments. They claim that it is impossible to ensure that the contributions and greater income be applied to the sectors with least resources and in aid of economic development.

"Consensus" as Means of Modifying a Power Structure

The benefits which participants derive from a trade transaction are the result of a process of negotiation whose success depends on the capacity of the different participants in the contract to fix terms which are mutually convenient. From this arises the tendency of seeing the economic order as a kind of "win or lose" game. Thus, in the trade game, the material and political power of the developed countries has allowed these countries to gain at the expense of the interests of the Third World.

Although this way of seeing the exchange situation between one type of economy and another is not strictly correct, it does seem an adequate basis on which to examine the conditions in which international trade operates. In practice, the demands for the revision of the world system are aimed at changing a structure in which the central powers occupy a predominant hierarchical position which allows them to extract the best advantage from any economic transactions with the periphery. That is, these demands represent an attempt to correct the inherent consequences of a balance of favorable forces which operate precisely in the interests of the developed world.

The favorite process followed to reach this goal has been the search for "consensus" relating to measures of readjustment. Such a research implies a willingness on the part of the industrial nations to make concessions, which means giving up at least part of the benefits reaped, by virtue of their strength, and, even, the acceptance of mechanisms and instruments which might speed up the weakening of this very same power.

It must be noted that our views are not intended to suggest a strategy of permanent frontal conflict in the process of struggling for more justice in international economic affairs. Fundamentally we must underline the need to make as cohesive as possible the movement supporting the aspirations of the backward regions and to give it the means of strengthening effectively its capacity to face up to the representatives of the interests of the center. Although it is true that developing countries have limited material and potential power, it is also true that to increase this in the two ways considered is not impossible. Without doubt, it is important to own certain resources, especially oil, although others can be mentioned such as bauxite, which are scarce in the industrialized economies. Such ownership implies political potential in the present international set-up, and opens up perspectives in the possibilities for action of the Third World. From this point of view assistance to poor or technically backward regions is not effective if it is given on the basis of charity, rather than with the recognition that those who have economic power also have something to gain; it is a question of these powerful groups' interests and not simply a moral problem. It is clear that to take advantage of these opportunities, there must be a minimum of homogeneity inside the periphery and, above all, the resolve to take all necessary action to make their demands heard, along with the real possibility of using the most adequate means.

For the same reasons, it would be very difficult to support any argument in favour of a NIEO, based on the demand for compensation due for past and present "exploitation," "injustices," or "discrimination." Although such phenomena are real and account for demand for a new order, they are not enough to make the rich countries responsive to the problem or move them to accept the measures demanded.

It is almost redundant to underline the predominance of the conflict of interests of different types, in the course of the long delayed negotiations which are supposed to be serving to review the system. In a world context, under pressure from different types of conflict, observations emerge on the possibility of finding viable alternatives for putting the new order into practice. These take the form of "win-win" games where everybody can benefit.

Meanwhile, the general picture is that "Western governments are sceptical of the majority of proposals put forward in the name of a new international economic order, and differ in their willingness to discuss them, and if necessary, to implement them."(13) When circumstances demand it, they show willingness to consider modest concessions in the expectation of securing assurance regarding their energy supplies at suitable prices, as well as guarantees for foreign investments, access to raw materials, and collaboration in their antiinflation policies or against environmental pollution. Examples of this line of behavior are the acceptance of measures which, without affecting market prices, stabilize the export income of the periphery, since in this way developing countries can import larger quantities of capital goods and raw materials, or the proposal put forward by Henry Kissinger to set up an International Resources Bank. To this we can add the inclination of multinational financial organizations, like the World Bank, to channel any loans made to the underdeveloped countries toward the production of raw materials and foodstuffs.

On the other hand, the positions taken by governments in the Third World are greatly affected by internal factors that limit their ability to take different attitudes, even when the international situation demands it.

Insufficient Homogeneity in the Third World

The ground covered by the Third World since its claims were first heard has been made possible by its coordinated and unified effort. Solidarity among member countries and their ability to act together have been much greater than could have been expected, given the objective factors working against this. Clearly, the Third World has been able to withstand objective conflicts, such as the increase in fuel prices, which had an enormous impact on the underdeveloped countries; it has also survived maneuvers designed to break its front.

The nations on the periphery are quite different from one another, not only in geographical terms, but also in relation to their levels of industrial development and availability of resources. This phenomenon limits their ability to weld together the kind of single block, with a single platform and single-minded action, which would substantially increase the periphery's negotiating strength.

Latin America is not only different from other developing regions, it has differences among the various countries which it includes, despite the many links which exist between them.

Apart from differences in size, natural resources, or stage of development, we must point to differences in political structures and the social base of those who hold power. This has had a negative effect on the majority of regional cooperation projects, and, in particular, on attempts at integration.

These disparities at the heart of the Third World have encouraged the setting up of special links with the rich countries, such as the Lome Convention, recently renewed. On the other hand, we tend lately to hear more public expression of such differences, especially in the various international organizations. At the Arusha meeting of the Group of 77, UNCTAD V, and the Havana Meeting of the Non-aligned Countries, differences were voiced, and it was noticeable that some countries in stages of intermediate development tended to follow separate lines.

The Spreading of Transnational Corporations

The spreading of transnational corporations in different sectors of the Latin American economies means a weakening of the states' ability to regulate and control the activities and decisions of agents operating in their countries, since, clearly, "the operating methods of foreign firms are different from domestic industry, due to the fact that they are less sensitive to local methods of persuasion and dissuasion."(14)

International exchange of basic products, as well as manufacturers, is controlled, to a significant extent, by multinational corporations. Furthermore, a substantial proportion of the flow of goods takes place within the firms concerned, to such an extent that the notions of "markets" and "foreign trade" should be modified. As an indication of this, it might be noted that, according to some estimates, 88.9 percent of imports by U.S. manufacturing subsidiaries comes from the firm's headquarters.(15) This has enabled firms to extend the practices of fixing "transfer prices," adjusted according to the interests of the companies themselves, as a method of tax evasion, avoiding exchange controls, and accumulating shares hidden abroad.

Each country will have to consider the restrictions on its ability to readjust its own exchange arrangements, which are derived from the control such firms have on the ownership of the means of exploiting the countries' natural resources, as well as of the finishing processes, transport, and marketing of their basic products. What happens is that the operations of the extractive industries are governed by the needs of foreign corporations, and not according to the needs and interests of the country which actually owns these natural resources.

One of the strategies open to the developing countries has been to renegotiate the conditions under which foreign investors operate and to nationalize deposits and industries. These measures, however, only enable partial changes since the multinationals retain their power over the distribution and marketing processes. Furthermore, it is the transnational corporations who control the supply of certain critical raw materials, technology, and the production of appropriate machinery and equipment.

The multinationals are strongly represented in the Latin American manufacturing sector, especially in those economies which have a high level of diversification of production. This phenomenon has played a decisive part in the direction and shaping of industrial development, tending toward the production of non-mass consumption goods, with very little vertical integration in the economy as a whole, highly dependent on imported factors of production which tend to be inefficient, concentrated, and whose dynamism is based on product differentiation and the introduction of new models more than on mass production and increasing returns to scale.

One of the distinctive features of the behavior of multinational corporations is their location in the modern sectors of the economy where high levels of imports are required and whose products are, preferably, aimed at the domestic market. In general, the average coefficient of foreign purchases by foreign consortia is higher than for domestic firms, and furthermore, these purchases come, in the main, from the multinational's countries of origin.

Another phenomenon which has been on the increase during the seventies is the setting up, in underdeveloped countries, of factories which take advantage of the huge differences in wages, a favorable political climate, or the lower cost of other production factors - energy and the lack of environmental pollution controls, for example. To take advantage of these opportunities, whole industrial processes or parts of them are transferred to the periphery, many of which require labor-intensive methods, such as assembly operations. In these cases it is difficult to talk of manufactured exports, since we are dealing more with the export of labor power incorporated in the reexported goods. These mechanisms are controlled by multinationals directly or through so-called "international subcontracting" arrangements, by means of which they provide the factors of production and, at the same time, the only demand.

Multinational corporations are unquestionably leaders in the industrial pattern of the region, since they form the nucleus of modern, dynamic industry. However, apart from internal distortions, they are the cause of a considerable commercial deficit which exerts heavy pressure on the foreign sector of Latin American economies. Only under special circumstances do they make an effort to place their products on the international market. Such action accords fundamentally with the global strategy and interests of the firms themselves, and not with the needs and concerns of the poor countries.

The transnational corporations control the supply of technology and capital goods through which a significant part of economic progress is achieved. To the problems stemming from this fact, and the costs incurred, we have to add the impact on foreign trade and the competitiveness of the receiver country. Technological progress is very slow in activities of special importance to the backward areas, as occurs, for example, in tropical agriculture. Furthermore, suppliers attempt to keep to themselves for as long as possible any knowledge innovations. Basically, they are distributed through their branches, in a "captive" form, and when they are acquired by national firms, their potential adaptation to the needs of the receiver and their use is subject to "restrictive clauses," which aim at preventing, among other things, the user from competing in the supplier's markets. In conclusion, disequilibrium in foreign trade and in the foreign sector as a whole are highly influenced by the increasing presence of foreign firms operating on an international scale.

Because of the way in which the corporations operate, corrective meaures must not only be based on foreign trade policies or those relating to the foreign sector in general. It is a question of changing the basis of the conditions under which multinationals operate and of affecting the combination of factors which determine their behavior.

Multinational corporations will try to prevent the implementation of measures which might alter the position they enjoy, and they have the power to do so. They have access to the governments of the central powers from whom they seek support to bring pressure to bear on the authorities of the countries on the periphery in which they operate. At the same time, they actively "interfere in the domestic affairs of the host country, even by means of bribery."(16)

When measures are taken to improve the terms under which the developing countries are linked to the developed nations, benefits do accrue not necessarily to the poor countries but to the multinational companies, which appropriate a significant share of them. It is, therefore, highly likely that such firms would be the principal beneficiaries of the results of action designed to expand the periphery's trade, such as, for example, a real increase in preferential tariffs allowing access to the markets of rich countries, or an open liberalization of reciprocal trading arrangements among the developing countries.

It is up to the national governments to use their power to ensure the community's control over the behavior, growth, and dynamism of multinational companies, as well as to take advantage, in the national interest, of the potential such firms have in terms of world trade. With the exception of certain countries, certain periods of time, or in relation to some activities - the automobile industry, energy - the governments of the region, in general, have not made use of the tools available to them which might effectively prevent the indiscriminate entry and controlling presence of foreign firms.

In recent years, some legislation has introduced measures which might modify several of their more negative practices, such as transfer of technology, the prohibition of restrictive clauses, the holding under local jurisdiction of any legal conflicts with foreign investors, or the signing of agreements linking multinationals' imports with export commitments. But, on the whole, these measures are concerned with partial aspects of the problem only, and have not managed to affect in any significant way the impact of the transnationals' share of the region's economy.

The international order, thanks to the action of the Third World, has been acknowledging the basic principles of the rights of states to bring foreign investors under domestic regulations and to direct their operations according to national economic and social development needs. The central issue, however, is whether governments have the will to implement these criteria, and find the means to make them effective. In this sense it is significant that little progress has been achieved on the negotiated adoption of the International Code of Conduct for Transnational Corporations.

Market Distortions and Inefficiencies

Many industrial nations oppose various NIEO principles, arguing that the existing market system is better than interventionism and directionism. From this starting point, they claim that it would be better to improve and strengthen the functioning of the forces which govern the actual market system and free exchange of goods, rather than face the risks and costs of restructuring the system and controlling transactions. In fact, these arguments come up in opposition to the signing of agreements aimed at increasing or stabilizing the price of goods exported from the periphery. Although they are more receptive of stabilizing measures, countries which make these arguments are still suspicious of the agreements by which prices are being adjusted.

Clearly, the market has not led to a more efficient allocation and social enjoyment of productive resources. This can be seen in the indiscriminate exploitation of nonrenewable resources, in environmental pollution, and in the persistence of serious unemployment, even in boom periods and inside the dynamic centers of the system itself. Even the industrialized countries recognize the need for intervention to defend certain activities or the income of certain sectors of the population, as, for example, in agriculture. For the developing countries, the market has been the vehicle transporting the cyclical movements from the center, in the guise of serious fluctuations in the prices of primary products. Furthermore, both nationally and internationally, market forces have accentuated inequalities of income and wealth distribution, and have forced productive resources into activities which satisfy the demands of strata where wealth is already concentrated. In conclusion, market forces generally serve the established power structure. The new order, therefore, as far as the developing world is concerned, must not be limited to measures aimed at liberalizing their trade and encouraging the spontaneous operation of the market.

The world markets for technology and the products of interest to the periphery are nowhere near conditions of perfect competition, being dominated by oligopolistic or monopolistic elements. Underdeveloped countries' exports face barriers derived from the structure of markets themselves, as well as the tariff restrictions of the center. In particular, manufactured exports are affected by product differentiation and the inefficiency of the production system which is forced to work below optimum production levels, meaning that this type of export is dependent on the possibility of obtaining exceptionally favorable conditions from the industrialized nations.

An easier access to the markets of the center would enable countries to take advantage of economies of scale and reductions in cost; nevertheless, other problems would survive. First, the size and cost of investment is very high and the most advanced technology must be available, which, together with the relatively long maturity time of investments, means that initiatives are left to the multinationals - with the repercussions discussed above - or the national public sector. Some countries on the periphery are more advanced than others in their industrialization process, enabling them to take a bigger share in the benefits available through tariff preferences. A means of overcoming these difficulties would be to grant differential levels of tariff preferences, but this would impose an element of friction in the developing world, and would mean an attack on the very spirit of the NIEO.

The raising of the international value of exports or an increase in the export income of a country are not the same as an increase in the income level and standard of living of the strata with least resources. Even the most faithful adherents of orthodoxy admit that market forces do not automatically solve this problem. This is not an issue which is beyond the scope of economics, since, as we have seen in Latin America, it is a condition of development itself, and the very essence of a renewed world system. Many international texts make this explicit, such as the Charter of Economic Rights and Duties of States, when it says that "every State has the prime responsibility of promoting the economic, social and cultural development of its people."

Revitalization of Protectionist Practices in the Developed Countries

Two main factors appear to encourage the reemergence of protectionist pressures in industrialized countries. One is the weakening and loss of efficiency of certain productive activites, both in finished goods and systems of production, in the face of competition from goods purchased on the periphery with lower labor costs. The outstanding examples are in textiles, clothing, timber, leather, and footwear; the problem is also felt in steel, paper, shipbuilding, and electrical goods industries. The various rounds of negotiations on tariff reductions have concentrated on the products exchanged by the industrialized economies, and, at the same time, a proliferation of nontariff measures has taken place, such as the intensification of the use of "safeguarding clauses" limiting the effect of preference systems. The developed countries are, therefore, tackling the need to set in motion a process of renewal and reorganization in certain areas of production which, without doubt, are the cause of serious social tensions. An example of this situation is to be found in the American footwear industry, where the total number employed dropped 70 percent between 1966 and 1976; in Europe, the textile industry - the biggest employer on the continent - has closed down at least 3,500 firms, with more than half a million workers unemployed, over the last five years and it is estimated that another million will lose their jobs before 1985. Similarly, the European shipbuilding industry handled 50 percent of world production in 1950, falling to only 37 percent in 1977. The European nations are now attempting to legitimize the imposition of "selective restrictions" on imports, while at the same time the United States is reverting to the implementation of "compensatory rights," with the same aim of limiting imports.

The other forerunner of protectionist practices is the recession just suffered by the majority of the industrialized countries, from which, in fact, they have not yet completely recovered, and which has meant significant levels of unemployment which have nothing to do with imports from the Third World.

The importance of disequilibria in the balance of trade and the current accounts of national balances of payments should also be considered, along with instability in the currency markets, as causes of action aimed at raising barriers to foreign trade. This might explain why, when considering the greater access of Latin American products to the U.S. market, of all the requirements this one is both the most important and the least likely to receive a satisfactory American response.

The Weakening of the NIEO in Latin America

The Latin American bourgeoisie have proposed a change in the focus of the accumulation process, and a redefinition of the conditions they operate under the world market, through the tightening and strengthening of their association with international capital. Under the doctrine of "comparative advantages" they are aiming at implementing a policy of drastically lowering protections in their domestic markets. The objective is to expose the productive system to the open competition of foreign capital, as a means of provoking a reallocation of productive resources as a function of the export trade. At the same time, the deliberate and heavy reduction of real wage levels is one of the key instruments used to produce an immediate contraction of domestic demand. Thus, the process of capital concentration and centralization is accelerated, while, at the same time, high unemployment appears. In this context, changes in the composition and dynamism of the export sector have to be seen fundamentally as the consequence of the lowering of wages and the inability of domestic markets to absorb the countries' production.

Such practices are incompatible with liberal-democratic institutions, and have required the setting up of the authoritarian and repressive regimes, which are to be seen in the Southern part of the region.

The content of these ideologies and the experiences they have offered are in open contradiction to the very notion of a new international order based on justice and solidarity. They have adopted a development style which depends on capital concentration and excludes the majority of society. Furthermore, they use strategies which are based on an adjustment of the periphery to the requirements of the central economies, rather than on the defense of national interests and the strengthening of regional cooperation, as well as cooperation with the developing world as a whole. The situation is reflected in the minor role played by Latin America in the present efforts to build a new order, after a long period in which the region had a leading role in the mobilization of the Third World.

A TRUE NEW WORLD ORDER IS IN CONSTRUCTION

The problems relating to the setting up of the NIEO cannot be seen in the context of an open struggle against the old order, which is resisting strongly. In fact, as a study of the Trilateral Commission admits, the international order created after World War II is no longer adequate for new conditions and needs, and "it broke down because of the essential changes which have taken place around its fundamental premises."(17)

What is at stake, therefore, is the ability of the Third World to direct the process of construction of the new system toward its own aspirations. It could be said, however, that although the claims of the developing nations contributed to a sharpening of the legitimacy crisis of the postwar order, they have not had the same success in shaping an effective, alternative model which could take the place of the system which is in crisis.

The evolution of the world economy shows important transformations, which indicate the lines along which a renewed order might differ from that put forward by UNCTAD and other organizations. Through the internationalization of the productive process and the spreading of industry, the developed world is attempting to move toward solutions demanded by the dynamics of its own models of accumulation. Multinational capital is the spearhead of this tendency, which means changes in the links between the periphery and the center. In fact, "the trilateral world has an increasing need for the developing countries as sources of raw materials, exports markets, and, most importantly, as constructive partners in the operations of an effective political and economic world order."(18) However, if an order is to be imposed which basically responds to the interests of the central economies, it would seem to be foolhardy to expect any qualitative change in the conditions of the poor countries, or any significant reduction in the gap which separates them from the industrialized world.

Table 5.1. Latin America: Trade Balance (Million dollars)

	Export of goods FOB			Import of goods FOB			Balance of goods			Net service payments (not factors)			Trade balance		
	1975	1976	1977[a]	1975	1976	1977[a]	1975	1976	1977[a]	1975	1976	1977[a]	1975	1976	1977[a]
Latin America	37,229	43,267	50,824	42,261	43,082	47,883	-5,041	185	2,941	-3,394	-3,634	-3,743	-8,415	-3,449	-862
Oil-Exporting Countries	12,226	13,653	14,273	8,395	10,009	12,419	3,811	3,644	1,854	-1,180	-1,565	-1,945	2,631	2,079	-91
Bolivia	462	568	849	515	562	644	-53	6	5	-87	-87	-111	-140	-81	-168
Ecuador	1,013	1,296	1,385	1,086	1,060	1,305	7	236	80	-192	-182	-267	-185	54	-187
Trinidad Tobago	1,899	2,370	2,337	1,413	1,843	1,683	486	527	654	64	-27	-8	550	500	846
Venezuela	8,852	9,419	9,902	5,461	6,544	8,787	3,371	2,875	1,115	-965	-1,269	-1,559	2,406	1,606	-444
Non Oil-Exporting Countries	25,014	29,614	36,551	33,866	33,073	35,464	-8,852	-3,459	1,087	-2,214	-2,069	-1,798	-11,085	-5,528	-711
Argentina	2,961	3,895	5,610	3,510	2,783	3,741	-549	1,112	1,869	-310	-89	-76	-859	1,043	1,793
Barbados	94	74	75	197	195	230	-103	-121	-155	64	55	58	-39	-86	-97
Brazil	8,512	9,908	12,139	12,052	12,282	11,999	-3,540	-2,294	140	-1,514	-1,780	-725	-5,054	-4,074	-1,545
Colombia	1,746	2,390	2,796	1,424	1,676	2,047	322	714	749	-183	-140	-70	139	574	670
Costa Rica	493	589	823	627	696	900	-134	-107	-77	-32	-34	-52	-166	-141	-129
Chile	1,570	2,077	2,180	1,577	1,412	2,030	-7	665	150	-288	-278	-300	-295	387	-150
El Salvador	533	751	976	550	646	830	-17	105	146	-74	-72	-147	-91	33	-1
Guatemala	641	794	1,145	672	905	1,141	-31	-111	4	-46	-35	-87	-77	-146	-83
Guyana	351	272	252	306	330	283	45	-58	-31	-44	-56	-53	1	-114	-84
Haiti	50	111	143	121	158	238	-41	-47	-95	-15	-25	-33	-56	-72	-128
Honduras	303	403	515	378	427	545	-70	-24	-30	-39	-42	-54	-109	-66	-84
Jamaica	809	660	798	970	791	730	-161	-131	68	-47	-61	-67	-268	-192	1
Mexico	3,484	3,978	4,781	6,292	5,859	5,326	-2,829	-1,881	-545	451	494	795	-2,377	-1,387	250
Nicaragua	375	542	655	482	498	654	-107	44	1	-40	-47	-68	-147	-3	-67
Panama	331	267	271	823	784	760	-492	-517	-489	351	359	402	-141	-158	-87
Paraguay	176	181	279	227	230	348	-51	-49	-69	-39	-38	-58	-90	-87	-127
Peru	1,291	1,381	1,726	2,389	2,100	2,164	-1,098	-739	-438	-250	-142	-119	-1,348	-881	-557
Dominican Republic	894	716	780	773	764	848	121	-48.	-68	-125	-121	-134	4	-169	-202
Uruguay	385	565	607	496	537	650	-111	28	-43	-34	-37	-10	-145	-9	-453

Source: CEPAL, Estudios Economicos de America Latina (1974-1977).

[a]Preliminary figures.

Table 5.2. Latin America: Balance of Payments (Million dollars)

	Trade balance			Net utilities and interest payments			Balance on current account			Movement of capital			Balance of payments before compensation		
	1975	1976	1977[b]	1975	1976	1977[b]	1975	1976	1977[b]	1975	1976	1977[b]	1975	1976	1977[b]
Latin America	-8,435	-1,449	-882	-5,846	-6,965	-7,780	-14,046	-10,087	-8,297	15,011	12,719	13,308	965	2,662	5,611
Oil-Exporting Countries	2,631	2,079	-91	-442	-411	-511	2,047	1,480	-815	1,041	-998	1,393	3,088	572	578
Bolivia	-140	-81	-106	-31	-50	-80	-167	-129	-183	128	185	215	-39	56	32
Ecuador	-185	54	-187	-161	-200	-231	-334	-133	-408	241	319	564	-93	186	156
Trinidad	550	500	646	-227	-266	-265	312	223	370	197	38	99	509	261	460
Tobago	2,406	1,606	-444	-23	105	65	2,236	1,519	-594	475	-1,450	515	2,711	69	-79
Venezuela															
Non Oil-Exporting Countries	-11,966	-5,528	-711	-5,404	-6,554	-7,269	-16,093	-11,537	-7,452	13,970	13,627	11,915	-2,123	2,090	4,413
Argentina	-859	1,043	1,793	-428	-450	-508	-1,281	616	1,317	602	-495	1,162	-679	121	2,479
Barbados	-39	-66	-97	10	-4	-6	-40	-58	-90	58	40	50	18	-16	-10
Brazil	-5,054	-4,074	-1,585	-1,794	-2,248	-2,700	-6,838	-6,317	-4,285	5,874	8,629	4,745	-964	2,312	460
Colombia	139	574	679	-262	-293	-299	-97	331	420	210	278	243	113	609	663
Costa Rica	-166	-141	-129	-61	-76	-87	-218	-206	-205	218	242	301	-	36	-96
Chile	-295	387	-150	-284	-357	-359	-578	24	-493	150	156	511	-423	180	18
El Salvador	-91	33	-1	-29	-41	-50	-95	19	-21	109	62	48	14	81	27
Guatemala	-77	-146	-	-66	-66	-81	-65	-5	-67	171	216	272	106	211	295
Guyana	1	-114	-84	-19	-20	-20	-21	-136	-106	71	33	110	50	-103	4
Haiti	-56	-72	-128	-7	-7	-9	-43	-48	-96	30	60	104	-13	12	8
Honduras	-109	-66	-84	-28	-56	-59	-132	-118	-138	186	157	170	54	39	32
Jamaica	-208	-192	1	-103	-115	-139	-283	-307	-128	214	47	144	-74	-260	16
Mexico	-2,377	-1,387	250	-1,817	-2,173	-2,186	-4,080	-3,423	-1,786	4,257	2,437	2,256	177	-986	470
Nicaragua	-147	-3	-67	-54	-73	-95	-195	-72	-154	233	95	128	38	23	-26
Panama	-141	-158	-87	-23	-33	-39	-175	-203	-141	152	220	141	-25	17	-
Paraguay	-90	-87	-127	-13	-12	-16	-94	-98	-141	123	158	251	29	40	110
Peru	-1,348	-881	-557	-242	-371	-426	-1,573	-1,233	-964	1,076	912	668	-497	-321	-296
Dominican Republic	-4	-169	-202	-93	-87	-125	-63	-221	-283	91	210	340	28	-11	57
Uruguay	-145	-9	-53	-71	-72	-67	-217	-82	-121	145	190	241	-72	108	120

Source: CEPAL, Estudios Economicos de America Latina (1974-1977).

[b]Preliminary figures.

Table 5.3. Latin American Manufactured Goods Exports from Subsidiaries with American Majority Holdings, 1976. (Million dollars)

	X To US	X To other destinations	X Total subsidiaries	X Total of country's manufactured goods	Subsidiaries' share %
Argentina	80	288	368	856	43.0
Brazil	169	314	483	3618	13.3
Chile	4	22	26	294	8.8
Columbia	17	88	105	181	58.0
Mexico	247	81	328	1218	26.9
Peru	5	40	45	137	32.8

SOURCE: Survey of Current Business, May 1978, Tables 5B and 5C (pp. 33-34): ECLA, Estudios Economicos de America Latina (1974-1977).

NOTES

(1) See, among others, Isaac Mimian, "Progreso tecnico e internacionalizacion del proceso productivo," duplicated by CIDE (Mexico, 1978); Raul Trajtenberg, Transnacionales y fuerza de trabajo en la periferia (Mexico: ILET, 1978).
(2) ECLA, Economic Study of Latin America 1977, p. 1109.
(3) Isaac, Mimian, "Progreso tecnico...".
(4) Armando Arancibia, "1973-78: La via chilena a la pauperizacion y la dependencia." Economia de America Latina 1 (September 1978): 61-110.
(5) See R. Cruz Miramontes, "El SGP en la ley de Comercio de 1974 de E.U.," Comercio Exterior 28 (1978): 114; and Kees Den Boer, "Preferencias generalizadas de la CEE y desarrollo en el Tercer Mundo y America Latina," Comercio Exterior 26 (1976): 582.
(6) See Cuadernos de CEPAL (ECLA), "La Coyuntura Internacional y El Sector Externo" (Number 7) y "Relaciones Comerciales, Crisis Monetaria e Integracion Economica en America Latina" (Number 4).
(7) GATT, Le Commerce International en 1977/78. (Geneva, 1978), p. 15.
(8) See, among others, Gonzalo Martner, "Las Asociaciones de Productores: nuevo instrumento de cooperacion entre los paises en desarrollo," Desarrollo Economico 63, (October-December 1976); Guy Erb, "Los productos basicos en el decenio de los 70," Comercio Exterior 26 (1976): 426-41; Alfredo Harvey and Horst Grebe, "Asociaciones de Productores en America Latina; nuevo mecanismo de politica comercial," Comercio Exterior 27 (1977): 150-160.
(9) See H. Hvem, "Les matieres premieres, les accords multilateraux et la structure du pouvoir economique," Tiers Monde. 66 (April 1976): 504.
(10) Use of U.S. Food Resources for Diplomatic Purposes - An Examination of the Issues. Prepared for the Committee on International Relations, U.S. House of Representatives, by the Congressional Research Service. Library of Congress. (Washington, 1977).
(11) For example, the United States imports less than 20 percent of the copper it needs.
(12) F. Ellis, "La valoracion de exportaciones y las transferencias entre companias dedicadas a la industria de exportacion del banano en Centroamerica," Estudios Sociales Centroamericanos, No. 22, January-April 1979, p. 241.
(13) This is one of the few things which even such a determined opponent of a NIEO as Nathaniel Leff agrees with "The New Economic Order Bad Economics Worse Politics," Foreign Policy 24 (1976): 202-217.

(14) Richard N. Cooper, "A New International Economic Order for Mutual Gain," *Foreign Policy* 26 (1977): 106.
(15) Quoted by Fernando Fajnzylber and Trinidad Martinez Tarrago, *Las Empresas Transnacionales* (Mexico: Fondo de Cultura Economica, 1976), p. 297.
(16) Richard Cooper, "A New International Economic Order...": 107.
(17) Richard Cooper, Karl Kaiser, and Kosaka Masataka, *Towards a Renovated International System* (New York: Trilateral Commission, 1977), p. 1.
(18) John Campbell, quoted by Carlos Rico in "Interdependencia y trilateralismo: origenes de una estrategia," *Cuadernos Semestrales*, No. 2-3 1978, p. 69.

6 The Caribbean Economy and the New International Economic Order

Kari Levitt-Polanyi

THE QUEST FOR ECONOMIC JUSTICE: SOVEREIGNTY OVER NATURAL RESOURCES

Two Caribbean countries, Guyana (population 770,000) and Jamaica (population 2,040,000), have, in recent years, played a role in the assertion of Third World demands for fairer terms of participation in the international economic system, of a significance far exceeding their small size and fragile economic structures. Conscious of the limitations of formal political sovereignty gained in the 1960s, both Guyana and Jamaica have in recent years pursued radical and nationalistic policies of self-reliant socialism. In foreign policy there has been a strong thrust toward diversification of external relations.

Official policy of both these Commonwealth countries is nonalignment with respect to the two major power blocs. The early 1970s saw the establishment of diplomatic relations with Cuba, the largest and economically most developed of the islands of the Caribbean Archipelago. This represents an important step in the reversal of the fragmentation which has characterized the Caribbean since its foundation by European settlers, pirates, planters, conquerors, and assorted adventurers.

Together with Cuba, Guyana and Jamaica were active participants in the 1973 Algiers Summit of Non-aligned States which gave birth to the historic Declaration and Programme of Action on the New International Economic Order adopted at the Sixth Special Session of the General Assembly of the United Nations in May 1974. To date, this document, together with the Charter of Economic Rights and Duties of States, marks a watershed in the relations between the industrialized powers and their former colonial possessions or spheres of economic influence. The catalyst was the successful mobilization of commodity power by the oil-exporting (OPEC) countries. The principal issue of 1974 was undoubtedly sovereignty over natural resources.

Bauxite Initiatives

In the early 1970s both Guyana and Jamaica moved to assert their sovereign rights with respect to the operations of the international bauxite-alumina industry in these two countries. The Caribbean at that time supplied some three quarters of American imports of bauxite and alumina. Jamaica was then the world's largest bauxite producer; and Guyana particularly smarted under the contrast between the poverty of its people and the wealth of Alcan, nourished since 1916 on the bauxite wealth of that country.

Guyana had requested a controlling interest in Alcan's large bauxite mining operations in 1970. When the company refused, the government in 1971 nationalized their properties to form Guybau, the only major state-operated bauxite company in the Third World. In 1976, the government of Guyana nationalized the much smaller Reynolds bauxite properties.

In 1974 the government of Jamaica, faced by a drastic deterioration in its balance-of-payments position due to rising import prices of several commodities, including oil, exercised its sovereignty by the unilateral legislation of a substantial production levy on all of the international bauxite-aluminum companies operating in that country. The levy resulted in a sixfold increase in bauxite revenues accruing to the government, and established the principle of indexation with respect to the selling price of aluminum.

This was accompanied by the formation of the International Bauxite Association (IBA), accounting for over 70 percent of world bauxite production, and headquartered in Jamaica. The IBA has helped producing countries to win and to maintain gains by exercising moral persuasion to prevent competitive price (tax) cutting between producer countries. In 1978, guidelines for the pricing of bauxite were agreed upon, based on the general principle of two percent of the realized aluminum price. (Thus, for example, a metal price of $.55 per lb. would yield $24.64 per long ton of bauxite. This price is somewhat less than Jamaica has been able to obtain.)

Although the rise in the cost of fuel has caused severe problems for countries such as Jamaica, which is obliged to import 97 percent of its energy requirements, and has moveover an exceptionally high per capita energy consumption, the government of Jamaica has consistently supported the efforts of the oil-producing countries to reverse a situation in which poor countries were supplying cheap energy for the continued enrichment of the industrialized countries.

The Post-1974 Recessions

Following the dramatic events of 1974, during which many commodity prices soared and acres of print were devoted to journalistic and official speculations concerning the supposed "commodity power" of the Third World procedures, there followed a chronic slowdown of economic growth in the industrialized countries. This has variously been diagnosed as stagflation, cyclical recession, or more deep-seated secular economic crisis.

Whatever the cause of the slowdown, there is no doubt that the climate for concession to Third World demands has seriously deteriorated. Very little progress has been made toward the implementation of the various declarations confirming the need for a New International Economic Order. Recent protective measures for agricultural and manufactured goods have made American markets even less accessible. While supporters and opponents debate the effects of a new international division of labor which, we are told, is resulting in a significant relocation of production facilities from industrialized to developing countries, the exports of most developing countries, including those of the Caribbean, remain essentially raw or crudely processed primary materials, sold in monopolistic markets (many sellers, few buyers), or produced and transferred by transnational corporations in accordance with global strategies of sourcing in search of long-term profit.

The deep-seated objective conditions which gave rise to the Declaration and Programme of Action on the NIEO are becoming ever more grave. Indebtedness is mounting, and in some cases, is aggravated by heavy devaluations. Deteriorating terms of trade for commodity producers continue to cut into the purchasing power of imports. Mounting energy costs expose energy and import-intensive industries of some underdeveloped countries to job destruction, as production grinds to a halt for lack of foreign exchange to purchase raw materials. These are but some of the dark clouds hanging over the Caribbean economies.

Balances of Payments Crises and the IMF Crunch

Since 1975, both Guyana and Jamaica have experienced particularly difficult economic conditions, including several years of negative real growth. (Jamaica's 1973-78 year-by-year real growth rates were -0.1,; -0.3; -1.0; -6.7; -4.0 percent). Both countries have had to negotiate with the IMF for balance-of-payments assistance and are now obliged to observe severe economic guidelines and tests demanded by the Fund. These have the effects of reducing government expenditure, raising taxation, abolishing subsidies, and generally diminishing the capacity of the public sector to stimulate the economy. By means of a combination of incomes policies and devaluations, real wages are programmed to fall, while profit margins are supposed to widen. The assumption would seem to be that the economy will respond by reallocating resources toward production for export markets. There is, however, very little basis for such an assumption, with the possible exception of the stimulation of the tourist industry in Jamaica.

The local business sector has traditionally operated in the domestic market in passive response to external injections of purchasing power related to boom conditions for the mineral export sector. Lower real wages, accompanied by rising levels of unemployment, will act to depress domestic purchasing powers; while endemic shortages place a premium on the easy profit of the speculator over the riskier undertaking of investment in productive activity.

As for exports, there are inhibiting factors: neither supply nor demand of traditional agricultural export commodities - sugar and bananas - is likely to be responsive to lower real wages; the mineral export sector is only marginally affected by devaluation; while exports of labor-intensive manufactures typically have a high import content of raw materials.

Thus it is unlikely that the fragile and dependent economies of the Caribbean will be able to respond positively to the heavy devaluation prescribed by the financiers of Washington.

The fact is that a strong economic and political squeeze, when applied to a small, open, fragile economy whose balance of payments is extremely sensitive to adverse developments in trade, prices, and capital flows, may reinforce rather than reverse cumulative reduction in real output. This is one more manifestation of the perverse mechanism of dependent underdevelopment, of the illogical or inverted structures imposed upon these economies during 400 years of colonial extraction of labor and wealth.

Indeed, the Caribbean countries exhibit some of the severest features of dependent underdevelopment to be found anywhere in the Third World. All these reasons, together with the existence of an articulate political culture, a strong labor organization, and a high level of educational attainment, endow the Caribbean with a perspective of structural continuity of incorporation into the world capitalist system from slavery and the sugar plantation to the present day. The local population, descended from unfree labor, is not and never has been in charge of its own affairs. The demand for a New International Economic Order is thus an assertion of the demand for the dismantling of neocolonial economic structures, both external and internal.

CARIBBEAN ECONOMY

The Caribbean as a geographic, historical, and cultural entity consists of the Archipelago of islands stretching from Cuba in the northwest to Trinidad-Tobago in the southeast, together with the mainland territories of Belize and the three Guianas (Guyana, Suriname, and Cayenne). The largest countries - Haiti, Dominican Republic, and Cuba - gained independence in the nineteenth century, while the smaller former British colonies of Jamaica, Trinidad-Tobago, Guyana, Barbados, Bahamas, Grenada, Dominicana, and St. Lucia did not achieve independence until the 1960s and 1970s. Suriname gained independence from the Netherlands in 1975. In addition to these, there are three remaining British Associated States (Antigua, St. Kitts, and St. Vincent); five British colonies (Belize, the Caymans, British Virgin Islands, and Montserrat, Turks and Caicos); the Netherland Antilles; and the French overseas departments of Martinique, Guadeloupe, and Cayenne. Four of the British territories are likely to become independent states within the next two years, thus increasing the present 12 independent nation states to a possible 16 full-fledged members of the United Nations. The total population of the Caribbean as here defined is 28 million and the land area is approximately half a million square miles.

Most of the islands are densely populated, with the important exception of the largest, Cuba. The mainland territories of Belize and the Guianas are by no means fully exploited, nor even fully explored in terms of possible mineral wealth. The region as a whole is well-endowed with agricultural and livestock resources, as well as industrial minerals of bauxite, nickel, copper, and petroleum and gas. Because of the evident geographic and political fragmentation, each individual country or territory has a skewed resource distribution, the more so the smaller it is.

A more self-reliant pattern of economic development necessitates regional economic integration, a process which started some ten years ago and has, to date, produced the Caribbean Community (CARICOM), composed of the Commonwealth Caribbean territories. It is hoped that CARICOM may, in time, expand beyond the political boundaries of the Commonwealth to embrace the independent countries of Suriname, the Dominican Republic, and Haiti, and furthermore develop relations of economic cooperation with Cuba and possibly the Netherlands Antilles. An important step toward the strengthening of lateral ties in the Caribbean was taken in 1975, when, at the initiative of Trinidad-Tobago, the Caribbean Development and Cooperation Committee (CDCC) of ECLA was formed comprising Bahamas, Cuba, Dominican Republic, Grenada, Guyana, Haiti, Jamaica, Suriname, and

Trinidad-Tob[illegible] h Associated States and the Netherlands A[illegible] mbers.

In contr[illegible] geographic and linguistic (Spanish, Eng[illegible] Dutch) fragmentation, the Caribbean has [illegible] orical and cultural legacy: the sugar plan[illegible] dentured labor, a heavy African input [illegible], and extreme external economic depend[illegible] gely been organized by European settlers[illegible] ts, and adventurers to produce what is [illegible] ed and, conversely, to aspire to consume[illegible] ly produced, Caribbean economy is an i[illegible] al structure which is perilously vulnerable [illegible] rnal factors.

Inverted, Illogical Economies

It is no wonder that Caribbean academics, technicians, and politicians have been so insistent that the key to economic decolonization must be a restructuring of Third World economies to create logical and indigenous systems of production which can create surpluses for export so as to make it possible to buy the things which cannot be produced locally. This is an imperative which cuts across questions of ideology, since nothing - so it is argued - can assure the capacity of the national economies to accumulate a surplus, secure from the constant erosion of export earnings by adverse terms of trade. The argument is simple: if the commodities which are exported have no value for one's own society, and are in fact developed to serve a need of the dominant metropolitan trading partner, then a deterioration of the terms of trade leaves one's country with a reduced quantum of real international purchasing power. Neither the export commodities nor the resouces which produce them can be switched to domestic use. This reflects a structural misallocation of the human and natural resources of the country.

Furthermore, insofar as import-substituting domestic industries have been instituted to make inappropriate products with imported manufactured intermediate goods, using labor-saving and energy-using metropolitan technologies, a deteriorating capacity to import is likely to result in idle capacity and unemployment, without stimulating any increase in domestic output. An inverted economy is thus locked into its illogical structure.

Extreme Dependent Underdevelopment

This export-propelled neocolonial state of affairs has, in the past, been politically viable because it is capable of producing impressive GDP growth when international conditions favor its export sector. Thus, average per capita incomes, both of politically dependent and independent countries of the Caribbean, are not low by Third World standards.

These averages, however, are artificial in the sense that income distribution in the wealthier Caribbean countries is severely inequitable, and unemployment rates are both high and rising. Thus the current overall unemployment rate in Jamaica is 24 percent, while youth unemployment is 54 percent in the 14-19 age group and 36 percent in the 20-24 age group. Recorded unemployment rates in other Caribbean countries vary from 15 to 30 percent. It is important to understand that these high rates of unemployment are not particularly the result of slow economic growth - although slow and negative growth rates certainly aggravate a bad unemployment situation.

Thus, when the Jamaican economy grew at an annual average rate of six percent throughout the 12-year period of the bauxite boom (1960-1972), employment grew less than half of one percent (0.45) per annum. Total employment in the growth industry (bauxite) was, however, a mere 7,000, constituting one percent of the labor force. The reason lies in the capital-intensive nature of modern mineral extraction and in substitution of capital for labor in other sectors. Moreover, while export-propelled growth of this type is capable of generating high growth rates of GDP, it typically produces balance-of-payments problems when export growth slackens. By the rule of the international development agencies, such middle income countries are, however, ineligible for concessional aid to deal with these externally generated crises.

All the countries of the Caribbean, with the exception of Cuba, are tightly integrated into the market economies of the industrialized countries of the North Atlantic. All of them depend on one of two major commodity exports, supplemented in some cases by a small number of minor commodity exports. With the single exception of the special case of Puerto Rico, exports of manufactured goods, other than crudely processed agricultural or mineral raw materials, are marginal in importance, and destined almost exclusively for the Caribbean regional market.

Thus, crude and refined petroleum products are 90 percent of Trinidad's export earnings; bauxite alumina and aluminum are 80 percent of Suriname's export earnings; bauxite, alumina, sugar, and rice 80 percent of Guyana's export earnings; and bauxite and alumina 74 percent of Jamaica's export earnings, with sugar and bananas contributing an additional 12 percent. Dependence on mineral and agricultural export commodities is reflected also in their substantial contributions to GDP: Trinidad: petroleum 48 percent, sugar and other export agriculture two percent, manufacturing, exclusive of petroleum products, only seven to eight percent; Jamaica: bauxite and alumina 11 percent; Suriname: bauxite, alumina, and aluminum 30 percent. It is self-evident that a cutback in demand by the international aluminum industry, whether for reasons of weakening market conditions or switching of sourcing, has an immediate effect on national income, government revenue, and the balance of payments. Thus, a reduction of 25 percent in bauxite production in Jamaica in 1975, followed by a further ten percent reduction in 1976, although followed by a ten percent increase in 1977, left plants operating at 60 to 90 percent of capacity. This situation has contributed considerably to present balance-of-payments problems. As for the traditional agricultural commodities, principally sugar and bananas, the situation is a chronic disaster area.

Adverse Terms of Trade

The overall vulnerability of Caribbean economy to external trade factors is reflected in the following movements in the terms of trade for Jamaica (table 6.1). With the obvious exception of Trinidad, the sole oil-exporting country of the region, these figures are probably not unrepresentative of the general situation in the Caribbean.

Table 6.1. Terms of Trade for Jamaica, 1970, 1974, and 1977.

Indices of Terms of Trade	1970	1974	1977
Net Barter Terms of Trade (Px Pm)	100	85.7	80.2
Gross Barter Terms of Trade (PM X)	100	72.9	64.3
Income Terms of Trade (Xp x pm)	100	106.3	74.4

While the volume of domestic exports of Jamaica declined by three percent between 1970 and 1977, the volume of imports declined by a catastrophic 40 percent. Principally because of the rising expense of essential fuel imports to provision the bauxite and other industries, as well as the basic transportation and electricity needs, Jamaica has now arrived at a situation where raw material imports preempts 66 percent of import expenditures, with fuel alone accounting for 28 percent of all the imports. Indeed, fuel imports are the only major category of imports whose volume has not been drastically reduced since 1972. Taking that year as 100, the volume index of imports for 1977 shows consumer nondurables 60.0, consumer durables 16.0, chemicals 61.5, manufactured raw materials 51.3, transport equipment 30.0, construction materials 42.4, and machinery and equipment 30.3. This reflects a continuous and large decline in construction activity, in capital formation, and in the output of the manufacturing industries.

While the economy has been running in reverse gear, with five years of real negative income growth, debt charges have been mounting. Debt service obligations to the public sector are currently estimated to constitute between 27 and 34 percent of export earnings. Adding this to the essential fuel bill of 25 to 28 percent of estimated export earnings, we arrive at a possible 52 to 62 percent of export earnings earmarked for debt service and fuel imports alone! This critical situation has blown up since the beginning of the decade; as recently as 1973, the public sector debt service ratio was only six percent and fuel costs were ten percent, for a total of 16 percent of export earnings.

While it is neither possible nor necessary for the purposes of this discussion to go into any further details concerning the problems which the Caribbean has encountered in the 1970s, we conclude with a passing reference to an underlying and crucial characteristic of dependence: extreme technological weakness. Given the structural vulnerability of economies which produce an insufficient quantity and variety of use values for the direct basic needs of their population, and given the underutilization of local raw materials and the underdeveloped state of indigenous technological innovation, this is yet another area in which present international economic institutions fail to protect and develop the requirements of Third World countries.

Index

About the Editors and Contributors

JORGE LOZOYA, Project Codirector for the NIEO at CEESTEM

JAIME ESTEVEZ, Project Research Coordinator at CEESTEM

ARMANDO ARANCIBIA, Centro de Investigacion y Docencia Economica, Mexico City

CARLOS ARRIOLA, El Colegio de Mexico

JORGE BERTINI, Asociacion de Economistas del Tercer Mundo, Mexico City

JORGE FONTANALS, CRESAL-UNESCO, Caracas

KARI LEVITT-POLANYI, University of the West Indies, Kingston

ENRIQUE OTEIZA, CRESAL-UNESCO, Caracas

FERNANDO PORTA, CRESAL-UNESCO, Caracas

JUAN CARLOS PORTANTIERO, Facultad Latinoamericana de Ciencias Sociales, Mexico City

MARC RIMEZ, Centro de Investigacion y Docencia Economica, Mexico City

SUSANA SCHKOLNIK, CRESAL-UNESCO, Caracas